# A Treasure Worth the Effort

by Dudley Hall

*Published by*
**Successful Christian Living Ministries**
**Euless, Texas**

Published by Successful Christian Living Ministries
P.O. Box 101, Euless, TX  76039-0101.

Editorial Services provided by David J. Swisher: % Lasting Impressions,
P.O. Box 695, Ozark, MO 65721.

Editorial Assistance by Sue Layman (Euless, TX).
Cover Design by Greg Steinle, Creative "Ad"itude (Euless, TX).
Text Design & Layout by Lasting Impressions (Ozark, MO).

ISBN 1-888946-02-4
Library of Congress Catalog Card Number: 96-68472

Printed in the United States of America.
First Printing: April 1996.

*The kingdom of heaven is like
treasure hidden in a field.*

*When a man found it,
he hid it again, and then
in his joy went and sold all he had
and bought that field.*

*Matthew 13:44*

# Contents

# 1 ▎ *A Treasure Awaits*

Every Monday we heard the same exhortation from the coach: "Men, you can't stay the same. You'll either be better after today or worse. It all depends on how you respond to the pressure. Let's go out and get better!" I got tired of hearing it. Sometimes I didn't care about getting better; I just wanted to survive practice.

He was right, you know -- we are either growing or regressing, and it depends a great deal on our response to what is happening around us. Our Heavenly Father wants us to grow up into men and women who will express His nature. Therefore, He is leading us into the pressure that causes us to extend beyond our limitations, so that we will discover the resources He has made available to us through giving us His life.

He motivates us by giving glimpses of life full grown in the man, Jesus of Nazareth. It is a life so superior in essence and expression that it would be worth all we have to trade in order to obtain it. That 'trading up' is the process of repenting that results in changed perspective, changed values, changed attitudes, and changed behavior. This is growth, and God values it highly.

## GROWTH IS GOOD

If growth is good, why does it hurt so much? The call to discipleship is a call to growth, and with this growth comes pain. As God molds and forms us into His workmanship, the discomfort we feel is actually a positive thing, as it will ultimately result in an object of great value to the Master. Pressure is a painful part of the purification process, but it's also the force that turns coal into diamonds.

For many who have been in religious circles for a long time, the words, "Grow up!" easily sound like a trite expression. We are constantly saying, "I just want to be like Him," yet when God intensifies the pressure to conform us to the image of His Son, we find ourselves fretting and even complaining about His work in our lives. Pressure is a positive thing. However, when responded to incorrectly or refused altogether, pressure causes intense anxiety and turns our pains inward. We then hurt ourselves and those around us.

As we look together at the life God offers, let us be sure to pause frequently along the way to examine our own attitudes and responses as well as those we think we see in others. It seems that most people desire progress, but want it without change. However agonizing it may be, we must press on to maturity. As we seek to possess His life, God will help us to respond as only He would. It's a package deal, just like the parable Jesus told of the man who found treasure hidden in a field.

# DISCOVERED TREASURE

Jesus compared the Kingdom of Heaven to this man's experience in Matthew, chapter 13: "*The kingdom of heaven is like treasure hidden in a field. When a man found it, he hid it again, and then in his joy went and sold all he had and bought that field*" (Matt. 13:44). Two things happened. First, he found the treasure and admired it. But then he took the second and most important step: he did whatever was necessary to possess it.

Many of us have caught a glimpse of the treasure and truly admired it. We've seen the unconquerable, insuppressible life of Jesus and said, "Wow, look at that! He stood in the face of demons, death, hell and accusation, and remained strong...what a life!" We have admired from afar the life of love, but have not possessed it. Like a man standing there saying, "What a treasure! I wish I had it," we haven't taken the necessary steps to possess it.

It would have seemed much simpler for the man in the parable to grab the treasure and avoid the heavy price tag of buying the field. Yet, it would not have been his to obtain, and would have required his stealing the benefit at no cost to himself. Jesus praised the man for selling all he had to buy the field. Was Jesus praising carelessness? Or wisdom? Discipleship always has a cost, and this man understood that the true value of the treasure field was in accepting the price of the field as part of the joy of the treasure.

I heard recently about a lady who had won the lottery in her state. When they asked her how she was going to spend her 40 million dollars, she said, "I'm going to buy a double-wide trailer on my *own* land." We might chuckle at that, considering that 40 million dollars would be enough to buy quite a few double-wide trailers. The woman had set her aspirations far too low. She was willing to settle for a much smaller treasure than was available to her. Most people either set their sights too low or try to grab the treasure without the price tag. Failing to conceive of the latent value available is like owning the field but never bothering to see if it held treasure. On the other hand, trying to grab the treasure without owning the field is sure to bring ultimate ruin.

Do we truly believe that the life of love is the superior life? Do we believe that love is the strongest power in the universe? If so, then whatever it takes, we must go after this life of love. It is more important than all the projects that deplete our time and energies. It is reserved for those who *sell with joy all that they have.*

## THE LIFE GOD OFFERS

The kind of life Jesus offers is one that never dies, never gives up, cares more for others than for self, doesn't strut, doesn't have a swelled head, isn't *me first* and doesn't fly off the handle. Sound familiar? It should. The definition of the life Jesus offers comes from a familiar

# A Treasure Worth the Effort

passage that should be a part of every Christian's life as well as memory. It is essential to Christian living.

It may very well be that our familiarity with this passage causes us to lose the value of I Corinthians, chapter 13. We think it is beautiful to be read at weddings, but we don't seem to understand that this is healthy, normal living. This is the life that was in Jesus Christ, and it is the life that is offered to those that come to Him. It is a life free from strife, stress, despair, fear and anxiety. To give us a fresh perspective on this familiar reading, let's read it in the words of Eugene Peterson, from his new paraphrase translation called The Message (NavPress 1993)[1]:

> *If I speak with human eloquence and angelic ecstasy but don't love, I'm nothing but the creaking of a rusty gate.*
>
> *If I speak God's Word with power, revealing all His mysteries and making everything plain as day, and if I have faith that says to a mountain, "Jump" and it jumps, but I don't love, I am nothing.*
>
> *If I give everything I own to the poor and even go to the stake to be burned as a martyr, but I don't love, I've gotten nowhere. So, no matter what I say, what I believe, and what I do, I'm bankrupt without love.*
>
> *Love never gives up.*
> *Love cares more for others than self.*
> *Love doesn't want what it doesn't have.*
> *Love doesn't strut,*
> *Doesn't have a swelled head,*

## A Treasure Awaits

*Doesn't force itself on others,*
*Isn't always "me first,"*
*Doesn't fly off the handle,*
*Doesn't keep score of the sins of others,*
*Doesn't revel when others grovel,*
*Takes pleasure in the flowering of truth,*
*Puts up with anything,*
*Trusts God always,*
*Always looks for the best,*
*Never looks back,*
*But keeps going to the end.*

*Love never dies. Inspired speech will be over some day; praying in tongues will end; understanding will reach its limit. We know only a portion of the truth, and what we say about God is always incomplete. But when the Complete arrives, our incompleteness will be canceled.*

*When I was an infant at my mother's breast, I gurgled and cooed like any infant. When I grew up, I left those infant ways for good.*

*We don't yet see things clearly. We're squinting in a fog, peering through a mist. But it won't be long before the weather clears and the sun shines bright! We'll see it all then, see it all as clearly as God sees us, knowing him directly just as he knows us!*
*But for right now, until that completeness, we have three things to do to lead us toward that consummation: Trust*

*steadily in God, hope unswervingly, love extravagantly. And the best of the three is love.*

*Go after a life of love as if your life depended on it--because it does.*

I Corinthians 13:1 - 14:1

If only we could believe that God *is* love, and that it is His very nature to give nothing but blessing, happiness, and benefit to His creatures! If He were to give anything else, it would not be love. The problem is not with God, then, but with our refusal to embrace this life of love. We've abandoned God's best to pursue our own ends...and left our soul extremely sick in the process.

## HEALING THE SICK SOUL

Sin, reduced to its initial impulse, is the spirit of the creature turned toward self...seeking to appease its own will rather than operate in love. The life God gave to man was far more excellent and beautiful than this, but sin's corruption has disastrous consequences.

When God created man, He placed within him something very powerful and motivational. It is the design of God that this force (desire) move man in the direction of his destiny. Desire can be evil or good according to the direction in which it is turned. God placed this desire within man with the intent that man would desire to love God and share His life. God deposited this desire in order to fulfill His purpose; He wanted it to cause man to trust Him and live in dependence upon Him.

## A Treasure Awaits

It was this desire turned wrong that got Adam and Eve into trouble. Their desire to be like God and to know what God knew is what the devil used against them. Satan lied to them, saying that if they would eat of the tree of the knowledge of good and evil, their desire would be fulfilled. As they did, they fell into sin and out of fellowship with God. Since then, man's insatiable desire has gone after itself and away from the life of love found in God.

In view of this, let's examine the two kinds of life discussed in James 3:

> *Who is wise and understanding among you? Let him show it by his good life, by deeds done in the humility that comes from wisdom. But if you harbor bitter envy and selfish ambition in your hearts, do not boast about it or deny the truth. Such "wisdom" does not come from heaven but is earthly, unspiritual, of the devil. For where you have envy and selfish ambition, there you find disorder and every evil practice.*
>
> *But the wisdom that comes from heaven is first of all pure; then peace-loving, considerate, submissive, full of mercy and good fruit, impartial and sincere. Peacemakers who sow in peace raise a harvest of righteousness.*

James 3:13-18

James continues in chapter 4 with an explanation of the conflict between desires -- the source of many of our problems:

# A Treasure Worth the Effort

*What causes fights and quarrels among you? Don't they come from your desires that battle within you? You want something but don't get it. You kill and covet, but you cannot have what you want. You quarrel and fight. You do not have, because you do not ask God. When you ask, you do not receive, because you ask with wrong motives, that you may spend what you get on your pleasures.*

James 4:1-3

God placed inside of us the motivational power that would lead us to follow Him and to know Him. When perverted, that desire expresses itself primarily in four ways: *covetousness, envy, pride* and *wrath*[2]. These are all the result of desire turned inward toward self instead of outward toward God.

*Covetousness*, the never-ending wanting, is the cause of many of the problems in a person's heart. It is the desire . that is always going after things it can't have, and is never satisfied with what it attains. Many people believe they have financial problems, when in reality they simply have a problem with covetousness...sick souls wanting things they can't have, searching for ways to get them, only to find that, once obtained, they do not satisfy the longings of their hearts. Covetousness robs us of our peace.

The second way desire turned toward self manifests is through *envy*. Envy is worse than covetousness, because envy not only wants to have what the other person has, but also wants to eliminate what the other person has. It is the cause of all the ill will, resentment and unloving behavior that disturbs us, because it cannot allow anything to interfere with its own self interests. Envy ensures that its agenda is the only one that is important and everything else must be submitted to it.

The third manifested form of misdirected desire is *pride*...the sad proof of our fall from something better than we are. It causes us to seek something higher than we possess. Pride exalts itself against all that is in God or man that will not help it get the place it desires. It is desire reaching for a higher, but misdirected state.

A fourth way in which the sick soul expresses itself is *wrath*. Wrath is the result of desire being contradicted; it is what comes out of us in order to get our agenda on the schedule. Note James' explanation: *"What causes quarrels and fights among you? Don't they come from your desires that battle within you?"* When we can't get what we want, we'll fight for it. As we jockey for position, we begin to engage in criticism, sarcasm, and cutting remarks. We look for ways to hurt the one who opposes us, so that our way can come forward.

These four--covetousness, envy, pride, and wrath--are the most damaging sicknesses of the soul. Until they are cured, there is nothing that can be done that will satisfy us, make us whole, or keep us from the strife and despair that wracks our soul.

We try to curb our covetousness with self-reliance, rigid rules, and vows of poverty. We try to control envy with rules and regulations, severe treatment of the body, and religious acts. We try to put down pride by practicing false humility. We try to get rid of wrath by acting like we love people when we really don't. There are many ways in which we try to solve these problems. However, the give-away, the obvious evidence that we are not succeeding, is that we continue to live in anxiety with no peace or joy, and our love is passionless and cold. We trade the treasure of intimacy with God for religious duty and resignation.

# CONCLUSION

You can have the treasure, if you will buy the land, but you cannot steal the treasure from the land. You cannot get what God offers, just the "good stuff," without buying the life of Jesus. You can have peace, prosperity and wholeness, only if you are willing to buy the life of love.

Christian maturity is found in living the life of love -- in not only following the example of Christ, but actually possessing His very life. This life God offers--free from strife, stress, despair and anxiety--is normal and healthy. Unfortunately, our unmet desires and our fallen ways lead us to turn inward rather than outward, leaving our souls sick and diseased. God wants to bring us out to a better way. Let us begin our journey toward maturity.

*Father, awaken us to the need for this life. May those of us who are tired of living by the lusts of the sick soul experience a birth of love in our hearts. God, turn our desires toward You. Amen.*

# A Treasure Awaits

## Treasure Hunt "Clues"
Ch. 1 -- A Treasure Awaits

1. Why do I have to go through hard times and struggles when I am trying to be a good Christian?  What am I doing wrong?

    Romans 5:1-5, 6:1-14      I Thessalonians 5:16-18
    Romans 8:28-38            James 1:2-12

2. I can handle it if things are sometimes difficult.  But why is there so much pain in all of it?

    Psalm 23                 Philippians 3:7-15
    Matthew 5:3-12           I Peter 1:3-7, 4:12-19

3. I don't understand the emphasis on selling everything in order to "gain" Christ.  Does God really want us to have anything?

    Psalm 19:7-11            Colossians 3:1-10
    Matthew 6:19-34          I Timothy 6:6-12
    Philippians 4:19

4. When the man sold all he had, he bought a field with treasure and ended up with more than when he started.  Does that mean God wants us to be rich?

    Psalm 62:10              Ephesians 1:3-23, 3:16-19
    Proverbs 20:15, 21:21    I Timothy 6:6-19
    Jeremiah 9:23

5. If I occasionally have strife, stress, despair or anxiety, does that mean I am abnormal and unhealthy?

    Genesis 45:1-20          Romans 8:28-29, 11:33-36
    Proverbs 3:5-6           James 1:13-18
    Isaiah 55:8-9            I Peter 5:6-11

# 2 ‖ *Understanding the Journey*

## PEACE AT RISK

Our culture today is desperately searching for answers. The stress level today seems higher than it has ever been. More people are suffering from stress-related disease than at any time in history. It seems that our culture requires more of us than we have energy to give. As a result, many are suffering from fatigue and depression. We simply are not equipped to handle life at its current pace.

Part of the difficulty is that our flesh was programmed with the world's software, but our spirit was programmed with God's. As a result, Christians today find themselves navigating a journey they barely understand. Although we inwardly sense a destination, our flesh is dominated by the system of values reflected in our culture and wants to act accordingly. Conflict is the inevitable result.

Our society is increasingly trying to rid itself of

absolutes; not recognizing God as Creator, and thus not acknowledging His right to set boundaries or declare absolutes. Humanism is the predominant religion and relativism is its philosophy. Basic relativism says that every person has the right to decide for himself what is right or wrong. The process involves rewriting history, resetting standards, and redefining once mutually agreed upon terms.

The people of Crete had similar difficulties. Situated on an island in the Mediterranean Sea, the Cretans had acquired the reputation of being liars. Their culture had no absolutes regarding truth and deception. In fact, it seems success in their culture was measured by degrees of deception. It is not difficult to identify with the Cretans because *our* culture, too, is becoming more and more infiltrated by deception.

# THE BIRTHPLACE OF CHANGE

I'm told that Hitler had a motto inscribed above the gate of Auschwitz that said, "I want to raise a generation without a conscience." The whole world rose up against that mentality and sought to end this man's zealous quest. Yet, that seems to be the mentality most prevalent in today's culture. Somehow we have arrived at a bitter animosity toward absolutes in life. If we are going to avoid watching the world spin out of control, we must establish some moral absolutes.

To the perverted, deviant culture of Crete, Paul introduced the gospel and left Titus behind to establish churches. Paul was helping this young pastor, Titus, to evaluate and confront his culture with truth. I think we can learn something from him.

> *Paul, a bondservant of God, and an apostle of Jesus Christ, for the faith of those chosen of God and the knowledge of the truth which is according to godliness, in the hope of eternal life, which God, who cannot lie, promised long ages ago, but at the proper time manifested, even His word, in the proclamation with which I was entrusted according to the commandment of God our Savior; to Titus, my true child in a common faith: Grace and peace from God the Father and Christ Jesus our Savior.*
>
> Titus 1:1-4 (NASB)

From this passage we can draw some practical imperatives.

### Know Whom You Represent

Paul was a representative of God. He said he was a bondservant...bought by God with allegiance to God alone. If you have been bought by, or have allegiance to, anything else, then your culture owns you. Paul also said that he was an Apostle of Jesus Christ...sent by Jesus. He didn't decide to go there himself to further his career, make more money, or receive applause. He was an Apostle, a sent one, of Jesus Christ.

Likewise, you must know whom you represent if you are to be an effective ambassador. You are either a *product of* your culture or a *prophet to* your culture. If your goal is to be a hero, you'll choose to champion the values of your culture. If you choose to be a change agent, you must adopt the values of God's Kingdom. You will never change your culture unless you know who owns you and who sent you. Otherwise, you will only become a part of promoting and prolonging the culture that exists.

## Know Your Target

Paul said that he had come "...*for the faith of those chosen of God and the knowledge of the truth which is according to godliness*" (v.1). Here we find two aspects of his target. First, he said he would change the culture by dealing with the faith of the chosen. Paul wasn't attempting to change the Cretan culture primarily through political action. That would be a by-product of hitting his target. People enlightened with Gospel truth get involved in every aspect of life.

But Paul's goal was, "*the faith of the chosen.*" The key to changing a culture is the chosen--the Church, the elect, the people of God. When their faith is built up, they can change things around them. They are the salt and light in the world. The second aspect of his target was "...*a knowledge of truth which is according to godliness.*" This is not a philosophical or theological knowledge of truth, but a knowledge of truth that changes behavior.

Truth that changes cultures is living truth that produces a superior lifestyle. This kind of truth is found only in one person in all of history. Jesus is the definition and expression of truth -- He is principles in living motion. He is absolute, but not static. Any system built on knowledge contrary to Him will fall.

## *Know Your Irreducibles*

What are "irreducibles"? Irreducibles are things you can't compromise. Paul describes them as "...*the hope of eternal life, which God, who cannot lie, promised long ages ago, but at the proper time manifested, even His word, in the proclamation with which I was entrusted according to the commandment of God our Savior*" (vv. 2-3).

There are a few absolute irreducibles that you can build your life around. First, there is a God...a God who is Sovereign, who is in charge. Second, this God cannot lie (an interesting statement to a Cretan-like culture)! Third, this God has spoken. That is powerful. If you can find out what God says, you've found truth. The truth search is over. Now the issue becomes obedience, not knowledge!

That, folks, is a solid bottom line: There is a God that cannot lie and He has spoken. When I receive what this God said, I have a basis for my value system. It doesn't matter what any government or organized religion says. I have a God who cannot lie. He has spoken through his creation, through Scripture, through the Incarnation, and through His Spirit. When I have heard what He has said, I have an absolute irreducible foundation upon which to build my life. If you don't have that foundation, you are building on shaky ground.

# CONQUERING THE ENEMY OF PEACE

When life gets heavy, it is usually because it is too complex. Simplicity comes from hearing the God who cannot lie. He gives us the real picture. Look at this capsule of truth Paul gave to Titus to equip him for the task of reflecting truth in the darkness of deception:

> *For the grace of God has appeared, bringing salvation to all men, instructing us to deny ungodliness and worldly desires and to live sensibly, righteously and godly in the present age, looking for the blessed hope and the appearing of the glory of our great God and Savior, Christ Jesus; who gave Himself for us, that He might redeem us from every lawless deed and purify for Himself a people for His own possession, zealous for good deeds.*
>
> Titus 2:11-13 (NASB)

We are encouraged by our culture to believe that our problems are a result of our lack of opportunity: we are 'victims in an unfair world.' We are told that our struggle is against injustice, and that we must demand our rights to our fair share. I am convinced the enemy of our peace is not a lack of respect, privilege, or wealth, but rather the unrelenting craving for these things. It should not surprise us that the world is frantically running the rat race to find something satisfying. The world has no steadfast anchor to hold them securely in the storms of life. But Christians should have some stability rather than constant defeat.

Some have simply denied their struggle. One way of

doing this is by surrendering to the world's value system. There is no struggle if you give in.  They have embraced their culture, concluding that everything is relative and there are no absolutes, so they don't have to struggle.  On the other hand, some deny that they have a struggle because they've been told it is unspiritual to struggle.  They are living in psychological denial, saying they have no problems...which in itself is a problem.

Perhaps your position is more like this: you are standing on the brink looking over at what the world offers, wishing you could have it but feeling guilty because you desire it.  Or, you may be secretly seeking some way to gain what the world offers while still maintaining your godliness.  That inner restlessness easily manifests itself as depression, stress  or frustration.  But you can simplify the struggle by recognizing your enemies.

## Recognize Your Enemies

Paul begins, *"For the grace of God has appeared, bringing salvation to all men, instructing us to deny ungodliness and worldly desires."*  I realize that "deny" is a word seldom welcomed in our society.  We don't like to deny ourselves anything.  And yet this may well be the reason we are in the mess I've just described.

### Deny Ungodliness

John Calvin is reported to have said, "Ungodliness is that which hinders sincere fear of God."  Let me give you a common, everyday word for ungodliness. It's selfishness... or self-centeredness.  Man was created in the image of God and was given great worth. He was conscious of God, the world and self. Self is a good thing, because without self you are nothing. We did not lose our value when man fell. We lost our stability and capacity to live selflessly. We lost our healthy sensitivity to God and the world.

Immediately after the Fall, Adam and Eve hid themselves because they became conscious of isolated self... they saw their nakedness and shame, and instantly experienced fear for the first time. Fear is what prevents godliness in many of our lives...fear of poverty, fear of humility and fear of obscurity. We are afraid that if God gets full control of our lives, He will make us poor. So we spend our lives, whether consciously of unconsciously, trying to pile up riches and resources so we will never be poor.

We are afraid that if we give our lives to God, He will humiliate us. Instead, He will humble us by revealing who we are and Who He Is. But when that happens, we end up with a greater sense of self-respect and are freed from the struggle for significance.

We are also afraid of the thought of living our lives in a place where nobody knows our name or appreciates our achievements. It is a scary thing, so we struggle for prominence. But when you become aware of your position in God's family and in His Kingdom, you don't fear the loss of temporary earthly prominence. Actually, the only way to eliminate the obsession with self is to replace it with an obsession for Jesus and a relationship with God through Him.

# A Treasure Worth the Effort

## Deny Worldly Desires

Worldly desires are the things we crave to alleviate all these fears. For instance, the craving for wealth is to satisfy the fear of poverty. The craving for notoriety seeks to alleviate the fear of humility. The craving for power and prominence is done to alleviate the fear of obscurity.

The world has a system of beliefs and values that is contrary to the Kingdom of God. If you don't deny these things, your fleshly self will rise up and become stronger and stronger. It will become such a nuisance to you that you cannot enjoy any manner of peace and victory in the Christian life. You must recognize that your obstacle--your enemy--is this fleshly soul that is programmed toward ungodliness and worldly desires.

## *Specify Your Objectives*

Notice carefully what Paul says in verse 12. "...*instructing us to deny ungodliness and worldly desires, and to live sensibly, righteously and godly in the present age.*" There are three important words here: sensibly, righteously, and godly. We need to reduce our pattern for living to these specific objectives.

Living sensibly is acting with proper stewardship of what God has entrusted to our care and patience in every situation. When it's all over, the man with the most toys does not win. Instead of craving what you *don't have*, you will concentrate on effectively using what you *do* have. When you live sensibly, God will give you more responsibility. Your motive is to be a faithful bondservant of God, sent by Jesus Christ to express the true nature of God the Father. Therefore, you steward everything He has given you to accomplish His assignment.

Living righteously, as old-fashioned as it may sound, is still a good thing. It means treating everyone justly, seeing that the other person gets what's due them, even if sometimes you do not. Righteous living means never defrauding anyone in any fashion. And if it comes to a choice, it means being willing to be defrauded yourself rather than let the other one suffer an injustice. Simply put, it's the attitude of the Lord Jesus.

Godly living is the opposite of selfish living. As we discussed earlier, self alone is not bad, but the focus on the elevation and protection of self...these are problems. We were programmed at the Fall with selfishness. Godly living is simply doing everything for the sake and glory of God. The new self God gave you at your new birth wants to give itself away. Giving is the nature of God. Therefore, to live godly...live generously. And in so doing, experience the joy of walking as He does.

# CONCLUSION

If you are honest, you will admit that even Christians have struggles in today's culture. In fact, I think that God has designed the struggle. But struggling does not imply that we must live in defeat. The issue is not with struggling to know God. Rather, it is this: because we know God, let's face the struggle and let Him show us the key to victory.

While we eagerly search, we can be sustained by

# A Treasure Worth the Effort

hope, that mysterious quality of eternal life that causes us to live in a higher perspective.  Verse 2:13 tells of our looking for the blessed hope of His appearing.  There's something wonderful in knowing that Jesus is coming back in fulfillment of all the prophecies and promises He has made.  At His appearing, the full payment of the inheritance (of which the Holy Spirit was simply a downpayment) will be given to us.  We will see Him in all His glory and realize that is what has motivated us all along.  Glory!

That hope of glory rejuvenates our faith.  The attitude of living with eternity in view helps counter the evils of our culture.  There will always be conflict.  But if you will isolate and identify your enemies...ungodliness and worldly desires, your task will be much simpler.  You will be trading up instead of down.  And if you will specify your objectives -- adopt the ones Paul offers -- you will receive incredible ability to withstand and overcome.

*Father, help us to deal with the reality of the struggle and rejoice in it. Teach us how to handle the enemies of our peace.  And lead us into walking according to Your objectives.*

*Amen.*

## *Treasure Hunt "Clues"*
### Ch. 2 -- Understanding the Journey

1. What do you mean "our flesh was programmed with the world's software, but our spirit was programmed with God's software"?

    Matthew 26:41　　　　　　　Titus 1:10-3:11,14
    Romans 8:1-14 **NASB　　　I Peter 1:13-25
    Romans 12:1-2

    ** NASB offers a more accurate rendering of "flesh" - the frailties of the
    human nature (i.e., carnally minded, fleshly minded).

2. If we have a right to choose, why does God have the right to set boundaries?

    Exodus 9:29, 15:18, 18:11　Acts 17:24
    Deuteronomy 10:14, 32:39　Romans 14:11
    I Chronicles 29:11-12　　　Hebrews 1:1-12
    Psalms 47, 50　　　　　　　Revelation 4:11
    Jeremiah 27:5

3. What does it really mean to be *in* the world and not *of* it?

    Job 21:11-15　　　　　　　Luke 8:14, 21:34
    Psalms 49:16-18　　　　　　Romans 12:1-2
    Proverbs 14:12, 15:21　　　Philippians 3:18
    Proverbs 23:20　　　　　　Colossians 3:2-5
    Matthew 6:25-34, 10:39

4. Why do you say that ungodliness is selfishness? Isn't ungodliness acts that are vile and evil?

    Proverbs 28:27　　　　　　Philippians 2:1-8
    Zechariah 7:4-6　　　　　　I Timothy 3:2-4
    I Corinthians 10:23-24　　　James 2:15-16

# 3 ❙  *Trading Up*

## THE CALL TO MATURITY

When I was a young boy, there was a particular area out behind the house where I built my sand castles and highways. I had my little cars, trucks and tractors. And when things got stressful for me, I can remember thinking, "If I could just get out to my sand bed." In *my* world, I controlled everything. That was a place to which I could retreat and find security and peace.

Later on, I had another such *program for happiness*. Down behind our house there was a holly tree that had grown out over a stream. I could walk out on that log, dangle my feet over the stream, and sit there listening to the gurgling of the brook, feeling the cool breeze. When things in high school became stressful, I would make my way down to the holly tree to sit and contemplate the world and my life, and find strategy there.

It is not unusual for children to set up these programs

for retreat. In some senses, it's a normal part of growing up. Those who study human development use the phrase "emotional programs for happiness" to describe these scenarios we create for ourselves that produce for us great happiness. At different levels of our growth, we have different programs. I would look a little silly now retreating to my sand bed when things got stressful. I must have a more mature program as I grow up.

All of us have emotional programs for happiness; we order our world in a way to produce the highest degree of happiness possible for us. The call to maturity often involves shedding the former programs in favor of a new and better way. This is a kind of repentance and growing up. We fight repentance, because it means giving up those things we have held onto as a means for producing our own happiness in order to gain new ones; and we have become attached to the old programs. Therein lies the tearing, uncomfortable nature of growth when we scream out, "Oh, it hurts!"

# FREEDOM FROM EMOTIONAL PROGRAMS

Maybe it would help if we had some clue where the goal is -- what are we growing toward? Let's state it like this: God is taking us to a maturity that allows us to love Him for His sake and to love others for their sake.

In the early stages of our relationship with God, we love God for our sake. We are self-centered, focused on our own needs, and we come to Him saying, "God help me!" That is not wrong, because ultimately God is Savior, and you are not going to come to God if you don't need a savior. Those who don't think they need a savior never really get to know God. It is okay for us to come to God with immature motives. God, however, wants to take us to the place where we are as free as Jesus was on the earth, as free as God Himself. He wants us to partake of His Divine nature (II Peter 1:4).

What does that mean? God wants us to love like He loves, and God loves for other's sake, not just for His own sake. God is seeking to take us beyond self-centeredness and manipulation to the place where we can love like He loves. To accomplish this, He has to destroy some of our emotional programs for happiness. Some of our idolatrous concepts of God, our limited definitions of reality, and other concepts that come from us rather than from Him must change.

Remember! God is in the business of presenting us with something so good and so big that we are willing to sell what we have, with joy, in order to get this treasure...to "trade up." We want to be at peace with God, walk in undefeatable joy and have the peace of God that passes understanding. We want that treasure. But unlike the man in Jesus' parable who sold all he had to buy the field where the treasure was hidden, we try to take the treasure without buying the field.

The field God wants us to buy is His whole life, not just the parts we choose for immediate personal benefits from it. If we want the treasure, we have to buy the field. That means giving up everything we have created for our own happiness, success and pleasure and receiving His program for our personal happiness. A big trade must be made.

## Exalting Him

There are several distinct types of emotional programs God wants to remove from our lives, one of which is the "notoriety syndrome." This involves being known and accepted by others as important. A good example of this is in Acts 8:9-24. Philip had gone to Samaria, and he was in the middle of a city-wide crusade, preaching the Kingdom of God and the name of Jesus. Great miracles were happening. One of the men who believed Philip's message was a magician named Simon.

Simon the Sorcerer had built his emotional program for happiness around his ability to mesmerize the people with his magic tricks. Evidently, he could do things that looked miraculous and people called him the Great Power of God. He had notoriety. The sound of our name on other people's lips is a very addictive thing, and Simon enjoyed being known and honored.

Then Philip came along, preaching the Kingdom of God and performing real miracles. Simon realized that Philip was not doing these things through trickery, but with real power greater than his own. He followed Philip everywhere, amazed at Philip's miracle ministry. When he saw that the Holy Spirit came upon people when the apostles laid their hands on them, he said, "I have got to have that." The key issue to ask is, "Why did he want this power? Was he interested in the ministry of God so that people could experience Jesus Christ and be set free from

# A Treasure Worth the Effort

their captivity to walk in the love of Christ?  Or was the reason that notoriety, popularity and esteem would be his if *he* could be the one whose touch caused the Spirit of God to come?

Simon the Sorcerer wanted the power of God in his life for popularity and notoriety's sake, because that is how he had learned to be happy.  He could not live without his name being spoken on other people's lips, crowds following him and men saying great things about him.

Today we still have the struggle of selfish ambition getting mixed up with our motives.  The answer is not in refusing the power of God for fear of somebody exalting our name, but in submitting to the discipline of God and exalting Him.  For true ministry to take place, we must desire the power of God in our lives for His glory and the benefit of those to whom we are ministering, not for our sakes.  If for notoriety's sake, then as Peter said to Simon, we have no part in the ministry of Christ.

It is interesting to note that we have no record that Simon ever moved from his "I want God for me" mentality. He was willing to pay money to get it, which meant he totally misunderstood the grace of God.  When Peter rebuked him and warned him to pray and seek the Lord's forgiveness, Simon's response was, "You pray for me, so that none of these bad things will happen to *me*." His focus was still on "me"! Here was a man who had developed an emotional program for happiness in ministry based on the applause and adoration of people.  Instead of being converted, exchanging his way of doing things for God's way, he had simply tried to take the Kingdom of God and use it for his own ends.  That is a dangerous thing.

There is a tendency in all of us to get our selfish ambitions mixed up with God's work. We find ourselves ministering for our sake, not for the sake of those who need it and not for the glory of God. When that is the case, we need to pray that God will forgive us for the very thought of it, and ask Him to take us on to a higher level.

## True Righteousness

Another area where the Father wants to replace our programs for happiness is in our standard of righteousness. All of us have a concept of what it means to be right with God and we strive to achieve this righteous ideal.

We tend to believe in God, but fear his pure judgement. We desperately seek to be reconciled to God, at least to appease Him. Even the atheist is seeking a way to deal with the possibility of a God who requires absolute responsibility. Each of us seeks out a program to satisfy our happiness in the area of a righteous standing before God.

Our example from Scripture is Saul (as Paul was called earlier in his life). Saul's concept of what it meant to be right with God was based on his religious training. He zealously defended his interpretation of truth to the point of destroying those who disagreed. The motivation behind this says, "I've paid a high price to develop my theology and my way of being right with God. When others do not agree with my definition of righteousness, I must defend it."

True righteousness that comes from faith in Jesus Christ never has to defend itself. Faith-righteousness is its own defense. Its freedom testifies loudly of its validity.

# A Treasure Worth the Effort

While there is a need to detect the wolves, the kind of zealousness that Saul had when he imprisoned and killed Christians, as he tried to wipe out the reputation of Jesus, is a self-righteousness that comes from a total misunderstanding of God and how to relate to Him. In Romans 10:1-4, Paul (the converted Saul) says,

> "Brothers, my heart's desire and prayer for the Israelites is that they may be saved. For I can testify about them that they are zealous for God, but their zeal is not based on knowledge. Since they did not know the righteousness that comes from God and sought to establish their own, they did not submit to God's righteousness. Christ is the end of the law so that there may be righteousness for everyone who believes."

The Jews wanted to be righteous, but their definition of righteousness was living according to *their* interpretation of the letter of the law. They did not understand that God had given the law to expose their sinfulness, so that their sinfulness would drive them to faith in Jesus where they could receive His righteousness. They thought that the rules and regulations were given to make them righteous. The New Testament, however, teaches us that if the law could make us righteous, then Jesus came in vain.

It is easy for us to fall into the same mentality that pre-converted Saul had. We believe that if we do the right things according to our religious tradition, then we are right with God. The dead give-away is that we still don't have His love in our hearts. We judge others who don't live by our standard, and we are compelled to defend our definition of righteousness against everyone who doesn't agree with us. We fail to demonstrate unconditional love and feel uncomfortable in the presence of sinners because we are unable to look past the external to see the heart. We have zeal, but it does not come from God.

Saul's misunderstanding also included the idea that he could achieve righteousness for himself through self-discipline. This belief causes us to look with indignation and disdain on those who don't live as we do. It is like the man who is disciplined in his eating who looks at the overweight man and thinks, "Shame on you. Just lose weight." Or the man who has no trouble getting up early and spending time reading the Bible who has disdain for the person who doesn't. This mentality can be applied to any good activity when it is done out of a motivation of trying to earn righteousness. If there's any contempt in our heart toward someone who does not agree with us or has not adopted our definition of righteousness, then we have an emotional program for being right with God that is going to have to be abandoned -- or at least adjusted.

Another aspect of Saul's misunderstanding of righteousness was his belief that righteousness included knowing truth that others didn't. Saul felt superior in his knowledge of God. The Jews had been privileged by God to have been given the law, the prophets, and the commands of God. God had given them laws to live by that he had not given any other nation in the earth, and these laws would develop a society that was superior to any other society in the world. God had chosen to give His revelation to Israel and to use them as an example to the world of what happens when a people belong to God and trust Him. But the Jews had begun to believe that it was their special privileges and revelations of God that made them righteous.

Saul evidently thought that, too. He thought that he had superior righteousness because of his superior knowledge. If we have any tendency to do this, we have a self-righteousness. Maybe it is because we have been in the "free-er" church, have been to more conferences, have read the right book or had a spiritual experience that others haven't. These feelings of superiority come from self-righteousness, not faith-righteousness. Fortunately, God will destroy that religious program for emotional happiness in order for us to grow up and learn to love for God's sake.

Paul's own account of his conversion -- given in his testimony before Festus and Felix (Acts 26) -- reveals much insight into his former perspective. On the Damascus Road, Paul's emotional program for his religious happiness was changed. You may want to re-read that account.

God is in the process of taking us to where we love God for God's sake and love others for other's sake. If that is not where you are, you have some adventurous growing ahead, and you can rejoice in it.

## CONCLUSION

God calls us to follow Him wholeheartedly and expects us to remove anything that hinders our relationship with Him. Our outgrown emotional programs for happiness hinder growth and must be eradicated. It is the process of exchanging our way of doing things for His way.

Trading up for the life of love is like the wise man's buying of the field to obtain the treasure. It will cost you all the outmoded, inadequate scenarios you have developed for your success. They don't work anyway. Trade them for His life of unconditional love. Is it too costly to give up your sickness to receive health?

**Father, make this truth real in our lives. Mature us into your design and bring us to a higher level. Amen.**

# A Treasure Worth the Effort

## *Treasure Hunt "Clues"*
Ch. 3 -- Trading Up

1. How is maturing a kind of repentance?

   Proverbs 9:6              I Corinthians 13:11-12
   Romans 6:1-14            I Peter 2:1-3

2. What were some of the idols in Scripture that may be in my life?

   Exodus 20:3-6,23         Luke 16:13
   I Samuel 15:23           Romans 1:18-32
   Psalms 106:36-43         I Corinthians 6:9-10
   Matthew 6:24             I Timothy 6:10

3. How can you get by in the real world if no one thinks you are important?

   Psalms 139
   Philippians 2:5-11
   I Peter 2:4-10, 5:6-11

4. How can I know my real motives?

   Psalms 139:23-24
   James 3:9 - 4:3,18

5. What do I do if I have wrong motives?

   Proverbs 28:13-14        James 1:19-25, 4:4-10
   Romans 8:26-27           I John 1:9

# 4 ‖ A Harvest of Righteousness and Peace

## GOD'S LOVING DISCIPLINE

To get a better understanding of how God moves us forward in maturity, we need to examine the message of Hebrews, chapter 12. The entire book of Hebrews is about moving on, going from the basics into the fullness of Christ's life. A major theme of Hebrews is the danger of neglecting your salvation--not taking advantage of opportunities to move on in relationship with God. In Hebrews 12, we are given instruction about the discipline of the Lord:

*...And you have forgotten that word of encouragement that addresses you as sons:*

*'My son, do not make light of the Lord's discipline, and do*

> *not lose heart when he rebukes*
> *you, because the Lord disciplines*
> *those He loves, and He punishes*
> *everyone He accepts as a son.'*
>
> *Endure hardship as discipline; God is*
> *treating you as sons...*
>
> *Our fathers disciplined us for a little*
> *while as they thought best: but God disciplines*
> *us for our good, that we may share in His*
> *holiness. No discipline seems pleasant at the*
> *time, but painful. Later on, however, it*
> *produces a harvest of righteousness and peace*
> *for those who have been trained by it.*
>
> *Therefore, strengthen your feeble arms*
> *and weak knees. 'Make level paths for your*
> *feet,' so that the lame may not be disabled, but*
> *rather healed.*
>
> Hebrews 12:5-7a, 10-13

When God is seeking to carry us on to the place of loving Him for His sake and loving others for others' sake, we begin to experience the discipline of the Lord. There are several things we can learn about the Father's discipline from this passage.

## The Encouragement of Discipline

Notice in verses 5-7a that discipline should be received as a word of encouragement. When God disciplines us, we need to see it as encouragement. How can we take pain, disillusionment, and disappointment as

# A Treasure Worth the Effort

encouragement?  From God's perspective (which He is showing us here), discipline shows that God loves us enough not to leave us wallowing in our own self-centeredness.  He wants to deliver us from our little world where we try to manipulate God, develop our own righteousness and control others in order to fulfill our programs for happiness.

God the Father is trying to get you out of your "sand bed" and into maturity, where you can actually live the life of Jesus--loving others for others' sake--rather than being defensive and always thinking about yourself.  It is true that God loves you just like you are.  The message here is that He *also* loves you too much to leave you there, so you need to take discipline as an encouragement.

The end result of discipline, according to Hebrews 12:10, is to achieve our good, that we may share in His holiness.  Sharing in his holiness means sharing in His life, His distinctiveness.   God is distinct in that He loves unconditionally, lives in mercy and is able to bless those who curse Him.  He looks beyond our flaws to see the ultimate good He is putting in our lives.  The undefeatable life (which is the life of love described in 1 Corinthians 13) is the life that the Father wants us to share.  He is seeking now to carry us on to that life.

### The Temporary Nature of Pain

There is another word given here that describes this process. Hebrews 12:11 says, *"No discipline seems pleasant at the time..."*  You need to underline that in your Bible. <u>Discipline does not seem to be pleasant</u>.  Those who have a theology which says God loves you so much He won't ever let you go through pain, disappointment, disillusionment, or suffering are going to have a rude awakening one day. Discipline, according to Scripture, does not seem to be joyous at the time.

The reason discipline seems only bad to us, is that we have built up emotional programs for happiness which rule our thoughts when severe stress and disappointment come our way. We like our programs because they usually meet our needs, and we don't like to give them up. As God puts us in a situation that reveals the inadequacy of what we have, it is indeed painful. That program for happiness has been giving us security, significance, peace and a reason to live. Now God is exposing its frailty. It's hard to convince ourselves this is good. It feels terrible. God is ripping away from us the thing we have relied on for security, but His purpose is good. Really, it is.

## *The Release of Inadequacy*

The process God uses in removing your emotional program for happiness is not difficult to understand. He leads you into a situation where your particular emotional program for happiness does not satisfy. Something happens in your life where your definition of God, faith, righteousness and peace is shattered. You thought it worked this way -- do the proper thing and get the prescribed result -- but it didn't happen.

When God begins this process, frustration and anger are usually the result, because now our emotional programs for happiness are not meeting our needs. When it doesn't work the way we've got it designed to work, then we become frustrated or angry. A simple example of this is driving in traffic. Someone cuts me off, does something risky, or breaks a law. I often find myself getting angry with a car. I don't know the driver. He or she could be a great person for all I know. But I know that I've just been cut off in traffic, and all of a sudden I'm frustrated and angry.

Do you know what has happened? My emotional program for happiness is that I get to do my own thing and nobody takes advantage of me. But when someone makes me alter my agenda and takes over the place on the highway that I have a right to, I feel mistreated and I become angry. That reaction happens because of my emotional program. So God, in His love, exposes not only my anger, but the focus that produced it.

Rather than berate me for being angry, God gently says, "Dudley, if you are wise, you'll see that this anger is pointing out that you have an inadequate emotional program for happiness for this situation. The only way you are going to get free is to accept my definition of happiness. Then your anger will leave." Blame, anger and frustration can all be symptoms of having an inadequate program for happiness. But God is looking to trade that for a better way of living life.

## OUR OWN DISCIPLINE WOUNDS US

A dangerous companion to improper emotional programs for happiness is woundedness. Woundedness is discipline turned inward (by us, not God); it is self-inflicted and deadly. When we are wounded we tend to develop an emotional program for happiness *amidst our pain.* Ultimately (if we are not careful), we will become victims-- happy with our sickness and our limitations.

Have you ever known someone who wasn't happy unless they were miserable? It is an easy trap to fall into. We find or create for ourselves a comfortable place in our misery, our self-pity and our depression (or oppression), refusing to be happy unless we are worried, angry or depressed. There are those who go around seeking to create trouble because they just cannot be happy unless trouble is brewing. This is not the superior life.

A good illustration for this woundedness-based program is Cain and Abel in Genesis chapter 4. Cain was a farmer and Abel was a sheep herder. God had revealed to both of them that He was a God of atonement, and when they came to worship Him they must bring an animal so that blood could be shed and substitution made.

This was because God has always been a God of "faith-righteousness". In other words, any person's righteousness has to come on the basis of a blood sacrifice, so an animal had to die. Life had to be given up, and blood had to be shed in order for sinful people to be able to come into the presence of God. Abel brought an animal, and it was slain in the presence of God, offered to God, and accepted by God.

Cain, however, did what seemed reasonable to him as a farmer; he brought his grain and offered it to God. He had his own plan, basically saying, "I'll worship God *my* way." He gave God a very costly offering, but it wasn't the

# A Treasure Worth the Effort

one God required and it violated God's very nature.

Cain revealed that he did not fully appreciate the holiness of God nor God's way of doing things. He brought the grain offering and went through the same religious exercise as Abel, but he did not sense God's pleasure, so in the midst of his wounding he began to pout.

God saw this and asked him why his countenance was fallen. This was a wonderful act of mercy on God's part. God didn't have to come to him and reveal that. Often when we are wounded we don't want anybody to tell us that we are wounded. It is easy to sympathize with Cain as we think of personal examples to authenticate it. When God tells us we are wounded, it is because He is trying to get us over it. It is mercy for Him to point it out to us.

Living with a fallen countenance is dangerous. All of us suffer disappointment, disillusionment or depression at times. It is a part of life and a part of the discipline process. However, to stay in woundedness, relish it and create a comfortable place in it is very dangerous. God gave Cain a stern warning about this potential. He said:

> *"Why are you angry? Why is your face downcast? If you do what is right, will you not be accepted? But if you do not do what is right, sin is crouching at your door; it desires to have you, but you must master it."*
>
> Genesis 4:6-7

In our woundedness, we are vulnerable to taking up offenses, blaming God, judging others harshly and believing things that are not true, all because of the pain that is inside of us. We must not deny our woundedness, but we must not continue to live there. We must not make a comfortable bed out of the pain of rejection.

God did not approve of Cain's worship because it was not right. But He did not eliminate Cain from the race because of this one failure. God's desire was to correct him, discipline him and carry him on to something better. Cain couldn't keep his former concept of worship, so God had to change his definitions of righteousness, worship, the holiness of God and atonement. All of these things needed to be redefined for Cain, and God was ready to do it for him. But Cain would not take the discipline and correction of God. He began with pouting and grumbling -- and ended up a murderer.

The same potential is there for us. We have done what we thought was reasonable. We did our act of worship and were very fervent in it. We lived by the rules as we interpreted them, but have not experienced the pleasure of God. The tendency in the midst of that woundedness is to become envious of others, and to become critical and grumble toward God.

If we start pouting and do not receive the mercy of God, then sin stands at the door, and that sin is the sin of murder. It can express itself in gossip, judgementalism, hatred, or jealousy. It can even express itself in dastardly deeds like physical murder, but the main thing it does is keep us from entering into the mercy of God. If we continue holding on to woundedness, we will ultimately be disabled.

# CONCLUSION

When life hasn't turned out the way we thought it should and God hasn't operated according to our ideas of faith, the tendency is to stay wounded, feeling sorry for ourselves because God didn't treat us right. That is the Cain syndrome: your countenance has fallen and you've become satisfied with it.

God offers an answer to the despondency of such inner turmoil: "*Therefore strengthen your feeble arms and weak knees. 'Make level paths for your feet,' so that the lame may not be disabled, but rather healed*" (Hebrews 12:12-13). You say, "If I could strengthen my feeble arms and weak knees, I wouldn't be in this shape." You can. Jesus went into a place one time, and there was a man with a withered hand. Jesus said to him, "*Stand up.*" The man was able to stand up. That was not the problem. Then Jesus said to him, "*Stretch forth your hand.*" It was a *promise-command*. Every command of Jesus is really a promise in disguise because when Jesus tells you to do something, He releases the grace to accomplish it.

When we believe the word God gives -- rather than continue looking at our situation -- then God watches over the word to perform what He spoke. So, when He says, "Strengthen your arms," that means you can. This is a promise from God, because God is telling you to do something that in your own ability you can't do. Trust Him and say, "Okay God, You said to do it, therefore it must be do-able." Then, *in His strength* and *by faith*, you stretch forth your arms and start working again.

Start using your hands for the glory of God, and God

will strengthen them. You will be just like the man with the withered hand...you will stretch forth your hand and it will be a miracle. He also says to strengthen your knees for walking. You've been wounded and are now paralyzed. So you sit around wondering, "Why, why, why," and God says, "Get up." You may very well think (or say), "I can't get up!" But get up anyway. In Jesus' Name, get up. It's a miracle! You trust God, God gives you strength, you act on His word, and God performs a miracle.

> *Father, teach us to love and not to despise your discipline. Help us to rejoice in what you are accomplishing in us, and thank you for affirming us as sons. Give us the initiative to look to you and be delivered from the bondage of woundedness. Thank you for your promise of strength!* **Amen.**

# A Treasure Worth the Effort

## *Treasure Hunt "Clues"*
### Ch. 4 -- A Harvest of Righteousness and Peace

1. I know scripture talks about discipline being good for us, but why does it have to be this way?

       Proverbs 19:18,20        James 1:12,17
       Psalms 18:30-34          Hebrews 12:1-13
       Isaiah 55:6-9

2. How can you say that pain is temporary when some situations last for years?

       Psalms 37:1-11,35-40
       Hebrews 10:35-37
       I Peter 3:7

3. Isn't it all right to feel wounded as long as I don't "stay there" too long or strike back at the one who wounded me?

       Proverbs 14:12           James 1:19-21
       Proverbs 15:13,15        I Peter 2:1-3
       Proverbs 17:22

4. What do blame, anger, and frustration reveal about the inadequacy of my emotional programs for happiness?

       Genesis 4:6-7            Proverbs 19:11
       Exodus 34:5-7            Philippians 3:13-14
       Proverbs 16:32           James 1:19-25

# 5 ∥ *The Way of Wisdom: No Shortcuts*

## CHOICES AND CONSEQUENCES

If I were to offer you a pill that was guaranteed to open your eyes to divine understanding, give you control over all your weaknesses, and grant you success with all your responsibilities, would you take it? Most of us would probably rush to be first in line. One of our basic vulnerabilities is an obsession with finding an effortless way to achieve our goals.

Since the Garden of Eden, Satan has been offering shortcuts and mankind has willingly tried them all. All of us have tried to find an easier way at one time or another. Indeed, each of the heroes of faith spoken of in Hebrews 11 could have chosen an easier route. But they instead chose to walk the way of God and suffer whatever consequences came their way because they would not accept less than the life God offers. As we look at what

God's Word says about His way, we need to ask ourselves, "Are we walking in the wisdom of the Lord, or have we ventured off on a shortcut?"

# THE WAY OF WISDOM

Scripture is full of passages that speak of wisdom and the way of God. Proverbs 3:13-26 gives a great list of *blessings that come <u>when wisdom is considered valuable</u>.* I encourage you to read it thoroughly:

> Profit
> Long life
> True riches and honor
> Pleasant ways
> Peace
> Life to the soul
> Security
> Courage
> Rest
> Protection

The way of the Lord is the way of wisdom. Proverbs encourages us (here and elsewhere) to pursue wisdom. But this concept is not limited to the Old Testament. The letter of James tells us we can ask for wisdom and receive it -- generously and without reproach -- by faith (James 1:2-8). James also makes a clear distinction between wisdom from God and wisdom from below.

> *Who among you is wise and understanding? Let him show by his good behavior his deeds in the gentleness of*

*wisdom. But if you have bitter jealousy and selfish ambition in your heart, do not be arrogant and so lie against the truth. This wisdom is not that which comes down from above, but is earthly, natural, demonic. For where jealousy and selfish ambition exist, there is disorder and every evil thing.*

*But the wisdom from above is first pure, then peaceable, gentle, reasonable, full of mercy and good fruits, unwavering, without hypocrisy. And the seed whose fruit is righteousness is sown in peace by those who make peace.*

James 3:13-18 (NASB)

# WISDOM ELIMINATES SHORTCUTS

Wisdom is God's way of handling life. Ever since Eve's encounter with Satan in the Garden of Eden, there has been an optional way of handling God's gift of life. Satan offered Eve the opportunity to be like God by eating of the tree of the knowledge of good and evil, a direct contradiction of God's way. Eve took the shortcut and experienced death (separation from God), and Adam followed. Ever since then, man has been infected with this bent toward taking the short cut and experiencing the same separation from God.

Today, we still think that we can find a short cut to knowledge, power, peace and abundant life. If you try to take a shortcut, you will experience death in some form. If there were ever an opportunity to take a shortcut, it would have been in the garden of Gethsemane when Jesus, the sinless Son of God prayed, asking if there were any other way besides the cross. The Father's eternal answer to Him (and to us), is that His way is always the way of the cross.

There are two kinds of wisdom. You are either tuned in to the wisdom from above or the wisdom from below. It is easy to tell which one you have by looking at the fruit of each. Are you struggling with jealousy, selfish ambition, confusion and other evil things? Then you are using the wrong wisdom. James says that the wisdom from below operates on sense knowledge alone (whatever comes in through the five senses). It is demonic. Remember, the devil's way is pleasure now, pay later.

I don't think we are taking seriously enough the way of the Lord. The "way of the Lord", sometimes called the "way of God" or the "way of righteousness", is found more than 500 times in the Bible. We can be sure, then, that it is something God considers fairly important. Jesus said, "*I am the way, the truth and the life*" (John 14:6). If we try to get to the truth other than God's way, it won't be truth when we get there. Let's look at some examples of typical shortcuts. Maybe we can see if we are trying to take a shortcut and avoid the wreck that would be coming ahead.

## *The Shortcut to Knowledge (Information)*

Ours is a knowledge-centered society. We applaud and pursue knowledge. Our lives are filled with more information than we know how to handle. Unfortunately, with all this knowledge and information, we lack the

# A Treasure Worth the Effort

wisdom to handle it properly. We have an information glut and a wisdom deficit.

Before modern inventions were developed, the only way you could exchange information was either to write a letter or talk face-to-face. Information was so precious that you only shared what demanded a reply. Now we receive tons of information that requires no response from us. We are often flooded with unasked for, unneeded, unreplied to information. Our information is devoid of context.

Why is this development significant? It has affected our response to God! We come to church, read the Bible, listen to tapes and gather spiritual information, but sit there as passively as when we watch the news. It makes no difference in our lives. We think we have knowledge when we have accumulated much information. When we can quote the best authors, even quote appropriate Scriptures, and know what everybody thinks...then we *think* we understand. The truth is we don't understand anything if we aren't doing it.

We say we want to know God, yet what we look for is more information. If you really want to get to know God, obey Him. That may sound simplistic, but obeying God is the height of faith, and faith pleases God. There is only one way to *know* God and that is to follow Him. There is only one way to *follow* him, and that is to trust Him. There is only one way to *trust* Him and that is to be obedient. Wisdom requires faithful obedience--one step at a time.

Where do we begin to follow the Lord in obedience? We can begin with the last thing He told us. Truth demands a response. It can be a foundational truth (*i.e.*, God is majestic). Our response is worship. It can be a specific command given in Scripture (*i.e.*, Honor your parents). Or it could be a quickening of our inner man by the Holy Spirit that prompts us to action.

## The Shortcut to Power (Experience)

We can learn how wisdom operates by watching Jesus' life, because He is the epitome of the wisdom of God. How did Jesus learn the way of God? Hebrews 5:8 says that Jesus learned obedience through the things He suffered. If that is how He learned obedience, then we can expect to learn it in the same way. We live in a religious society that does not easily permit suffering. The assumption is that if you suffer it must be because you have sinned, and therefore are bad and worthy of rejection. We think that if we can obtain enough knowledge, we won't sin or suffer anymore.

Suffering doesn't fit into our comfortable, context-free, information society. We don't like to suffer or have to wait for what we want. We don't like processes, we want instant cures. God's way, however, is the way of patience: *"It is with faith and patience that you inherit the promise"* (Hebrews 6:12). There is a frightening vulnerability today in the Church. People are so hungry they will eat the junk food of shallow experience instead of the health food of God's processes.

God wants us to have power more than we want power. He wants us to understand our authority in the name of Jesus and to experience the power of the Holy

Spirit. God wants us operating in the actual power of resurrected life. That is why Paul prayed in Ephesians 1:17-20 that we would have such a spirit of wisdom and revelation in the knowledge of Him, that we would understand the exceeding power that works in us, which is the same power that raised Jesus from the dead. It is God's will for us to operate in that power, but it is not God's will for us to get more power than we have character.

Those who go for their inheritance before it is time always wind up in a hog pen. The prodigal son in Luke 15 came too early and said to his father, "I want my inheritance now." His father gave it to him and the son abused it and lost it, winding up in a hog pen. Today we see so many grasping for their inheritance before they have enough character to know what to do with it. God leads us through these processes because He is developing in us the ability to handle what He wants to give to us.

## GOD'S WAY TO WISDOM

The way of God is the way of faith: "*Without faith it is impossible to please God*" (Hebrews 11:6a). "*Everything that does not come from faith is sin*" (Romans 14:23b). God has guaranteed that all of His ways will be orchestrated by faith. This means that at some point we have to trust God. Whatever your goal is, whether it be knowledge, power, peace, victory or anything else, you are going to have to trust God in the process of attaining it.

Faith grows out of an ongoing, following, trusting relationship with Jesus. It's not just in events, it is in following Him every day -- even when you don't feel His presence as strongly as at other times.

Faith also implies death. Because of man's fallen state, the only way to get God's way done is to start over, and that requires death. That's the bad news. The good news of the cross is that there's nothing wrong with you that dying won't fix. After the cross comes the resurrection, which brings life, but first the old life must be put to death. In every event of your life, God's way will always lead you to death, burial, and resurrection of the promise. And the end result is always far more glorious than the first.

The way of God is the way of obedience. In today's freedom-filled atmosphere, obedience is not a popular word. Does it involve a return to working for righteousness? No. We are talking about living the life we already have. The life of grace -- the life of Jesus -- this beautiful, victorious life is lived by following the ways of God. This is living truth. This is love expressing itself in deeds and faith producing works.

You can be sure, however, that for every command God makes, He has already provided the means to obey. God always has a "ram in the bush" for a man who is full of faith. According to Hebrews 11:17-19, Abraham went up the mountain fully expecting to sacrifice his son Isaac, believing that God would then raise him from the dead. That is extraordinary faith. But Isaac's deliverance came through the ram. God won't always act in the way you think He will, but His way will always be better than our way. Believing that is the risk and adventure of obedience.

# A Treasure Worth the Effort

## CONCLUSION

Aren't you glad God didn't just give us life and leave us to figure out the best way to live it? He gave us life, and then He gave us the way. Although His way isn't necessarily the most obvious, and certainly is not the most popular, it can be found by the one who steadfastly seeks after the life God offers. When we pursue wisdom, we will find our heart's desire. That commitment will give us real joy, and we won't waste our lives on a shortcut that only leads to a dead-end.

You might want to re-evaluate this business of following Jesus, because the way of the Lord is the way of the cross, and that means death to everything you alone can produce. It is the only way you can really have life. You have to trust God to get it done. Our seeking is often extremely shallow, especially when we focus on things. God is indeed interested in what interests you, but if you are going to follow Him into the depths of knowing Him, He will also take you into the depths of your own heart. You will find things there that need to die -- things you didn't even know were supposed to die. Wisdom has a cross, and the way of the cross leads home to the Father.

*Father, thank you for demonstrating Your Way for us. Lead us into the depths of Your Truth, and keep us from settling for the all too familiar shortcuts. Your way of wisdom is best.* **Amen.**

## *Treasure Hunt "Clues"*
### Ch. 5 -- The Way of Wisdom: No Shortcuts

1. What does Scripture say about faith -- its results and/or consequences?

   II Corinthians 5:7          Ephesians 2:8-10
   Romans 1:17, 3:21-31        Hebrews 11
   Romans 8:18-27

2. How do I get wisdom?

   Proverbs 1:2-7a
   Proverbs 4:10-14
   James 1:5-6

3. How can I distinguish between wisdom from above and earthly wisdom?

   Proverbs 8:12-35, 9:9-10
   I Corinthians 2:6-16
   James 3:13-18

4. Why is wisdom so important?

   Proverbs 2, 3:1-26
   Proverbs 4:5-9, 16:16
   Colossians 2:2-3

# 6 ‖ *The Joy of Commitment*

## MORE THAN RECOMMITMENT

When I was growing up, I often heard it said in various ways that the problem with the church was the lack of commitment. I took that to heart. When I encountered problems in my life, I concluded the problem was that I wasn't committed enough, so I either meandered along in my lack of commitment (and the guilt that came with it), or, like many others, I 'recommitted' my life to the Lord.

On several occasions I walked down the aisle of a church, youth camp, or retreat center and recommitted myself to the Lord. Most of the time I didn't see much long-term benefit. The recommitment was simply a shoring up of my will power -- promising to do better (for a time). Ultimately, I didn't see much transformation taking place.

## The Joy of Commitment

Today, commitment has become a concept that is met with disdain. In the spiritually correct church where creative freedom reigns supreme, commitment is a forbidden concept. Is there a still a place for commitment or is it a treatise of a bygone era? Nothing of any eternal (or even long-term) value ever came about apart from commitment. Commitment is an essential part of the human experience.

We need to revisit this abandoned principle before we can proceed further. For the context in which I will use the word, here is a working definition: Commitment is a choice to invest with the hope of a significant return. The principle by which commitment works is this: Your return is based on your investment. Jesus said to his disciples:

> *If anyone comes to me and does not hate his father and mother, his wife and children, his brothers and sisters - yes, even his own life - he cannot be my disciple.*
> Luke 14:26

Jesus asks for total commitment. What is the return on this investment? Peter said to Jesus, *"We have left everything to follow you! What then will there be for us?"* (Matthew 19:27). Jesus responded, *"Everyone who has left houses or brothers or sisters or father or mother or children or fields for my sake will receive a hundred times as much and will inherit eternal life"* (Matthew 19:29).

A hundred fold return is a good return. Such a return should encourage you to make a commitment. However, we need to remember it works both ways -- a good investment reaps a good return, but a bad investment reaps a bad return. This is a biblical principle that appears in a number of places. For example:

> *Do not be deceived: God cannot be mocked. A man reaps what he sows. The one who sows to please his sinful nature, from that nature will reap destruction; the one who sows to please the Spirit, from the Spirit will reap eternal life.*
>
> Galatians 6:7-8

## FEAR HOLDS US BACK

There is something inside fallen man which does not want to lose the illusion of freedom that he has. As a result, we tend to fear commitment. Many people say, "I'm afraid to make a commitment because I don't think I can live up to it." Often, what they are really saying is, "I want my options open. I don't want to commit because that draws the lines." Therefore, they live in this nebulous sense of freedom that doesn't really exist.

This is true among casual Christians as well. They avoid making a commitment to be a responsible team member, because it cuts down on their options. They want the back door left open. Maybe those who do not enjoy living under a love that constrains them, never learned to live by a fear of consequences that restrained them.

Living under rules and regulations for fear of the consequences is not wrong; it's simply the beginning. That's what law is for. God, however, wants to propel you from living by a restraining fear to embracing a constraining love.

## The Joy of Commitment

The goal is compulsion by love. When you truly love someone, you'll break your neck trying to keep from doing anything to wreck the relationship or harm them.

Many of us have made commitments in the past that did not produce a viable return on our investment. Our fear of (past) failures holds us back. A great number of disillusioned Christians today were truly committed to a Sunday school -- thinking it would help them know God -- but instead settled for a lot of Bible verses and elementary principles. Others sold out to cell groups -- hoping to find loving nurture -- and instead found what they considered to be a group of sick, hurting people sharing their problems and discussing things they knew nothing about.

Unfortunately, commitment to their concept of church didn't meet their needs because it was destined to fail. If you still think that God, Christianity, and the Church exist to make you feel better about yourself and solve your problems, you will be disappointed in your commitments. If you are committed to a God like that, He won't perform. If you are committed to a church for that reason, it will not meet your needs.

The pain of failed commitments -- to things that did not perform up to our expectations -- has caused many of us to decide not to commit to anything. Many don't even attend church anymore. I am amazed at how many people I meet who tell me that at one time they were active church members, but they never intend to go back. People are basically saying, "I found out people are imperfect, and God won't act the way I want Him to act. Therefore, I am afraid to commit because I am afraid I will get hurt again."

Another obstacle to commitment is the fear of exposure. We fear that commitment to others will involve exposing our weaknesses. Let's say that I am a person who is habitually late. I generally show up late, but I reason that you should be glad to have me there at all, no matter how late it is when I get there. If we get together in some kind of covenant relationship, it won't be long before my tardiness and attitude is going to be exposed -- it will irritate somebody and there will be a conflict. So to avoid this exposure, I just won't make any commitments. But I don't get the maturity that confronting my problem would bring. No investment, no return!

Lawlessness is another obstacle -- living in such a way so as to avoid confinement, restrictions, and all forms of governmental control (including God's). Until it is brought to the Cross, it will express itself either religiously or non-religiously in terms of "liberty" and "freedom." In reality, it is nothing more than lawlessness. Because of our fallenness, it is a major stronghold in culture. To the degree that the culture affects our Christianity, we will be affected by this spirit of lawlessness: *"For the secret power of lawlessness is already at work..."* (II Thessalonians 2:7a).

# COMMITMENT MATTERS TO GOD

Commitment is essential, partly because it fits our nature. God, who made us in His image, is a covenant God; living in covenant requires commitment. In God's covenant with Abraham, He promised to bless Abraham and make him the father of many nations; to bless those that blessed him, and curse those that cursed him. This was God's commitment to Abraham. In return, He asked Abraham to believe the promises.

Because we are created in God's image, commitment is essential to our very nature. Any man not living in covenant with God and his fellow man is living in contradiction to how he was designed. He cannot find satisfaction or fulfillment, because he is attempting to obtain that which God does not offer.

As Christians, we are called members of the Body of Christ. In a physical body, the parts are all essential and interrelated. What's more, every part is committed to the head and to each other. God was trying to tell us something! As a part of a whole, our commitment is essential to the rest of the body. Attempting to live in isolated independence is a violation of God's nature.

Commitment is also essential because true commitment, when done properly, forces our maturity. It forces us to face our weaknesses. As we interact with God, His mercy extends to the point of our failures and weakness. As we live in relationship with other people, we learn Christian virtues we could not grasp elsewhere. When our weaknesses are exposed, we can find His strengths.

All the reciprocal commands of the New Testament are unnecessary unless we are living in some kind of commitment. If I am free to walk away when I choose to, with no pain or penalty, then I will not have my weaknesses exposed or be forced to grow beyond them. Commitment to God and to His people requires choosing to live with different and difficult people. Forgiveness, tolerance, cooperation and more are learned in that setting.

# A Treasure Worth the Effort

G. K. Chesterton had an excellent observation about the value of living in relationship with a small group, as opposed to living in the nebulous crowd:

> "It is not fashionable to say much nowadays about the advantages of the small community. We are told that we must go in for large empires, large ideas. There is one advantage, however, to the small state, the city, or the village which only the willfully blind can overlook. The man who lives in a small community lives in a much larger world. He knows much more about the fierce varieties and uncompromising divergences of men. The reason is obvious. In a large community, we can choose our companions. In a small community, our companions are chosen for us. Thus, in all extensive and highly civilized societies, groups come into existence founded upon what is called sympathy, and shut out the real world more sharply than the gates of a monastery."[3]

In an age of comfort, convenience, isolation and independence, we have lost the value of commitment to the small group. Yet, despite our culture's opposition, it is in this setting that God intends for us to flourish.

Commitment is necessary if we are to fulfill our destiny. The ultimate destiny of man is to worship God, and to steward the world under God's government. The principle by which we are to do that is: God gives you a little bit, and as you demonstrate faithfulness in it (doing it His way), He entrusts more to you. This requires unyielding commitment. Apart from commitment, there is no discipleship; and without discipleship there can be no real knowledge of God.

# TO WHOM AND WHAT DO WE COMMIT?

We are called to be committed to Jesus Christ Himself -- not just His teaching, not just an imitation of His life -- but to Him...to know Him and follow Him. This must be kept first and foremost. He is a vast treasure, and however deep you have gone with Him, you have not even touched the surface of that treasure. The more you drink from this fountain, the fuller and "thirstier" you get.

We are also called to be committed to Christ's Kingdom. There is a reality that exists beyond the kingdom we tend to live in -- the material, the temporal, what our physical eyes can see -- and that is the Kingdom of God. The Kingdom of God is not color-blind, it is colorful! And the Church is to be a place where differences come together so we can learn and grow.

That brings us to the next thing we are called to commit ourselves to -- Christ's Church. While the Kingdom is the essence of government and the reality of God, the Church is the expression of the Kingdom on the earth. You cannot be committed to the invisible Kingdom if you are not a part of God's plan to make that Kingdom visible on the earth through the Church. That is the way God designed it. You will discover your own significance only as you relate in mutual submission to the body of Christ.

This commitment process must be kept in order. To

commit to the Kingdom first will make you a hard-nosed crusader for re-establishing Biblical law in society. To commit to His Church first inevitably produces ecclesiastical Pharisees who ignore the world while they tinker with church structures and doctrine.

To place the Church above the Kingdom creates protectionism and self-preservation among church leaders. It results in division and deception as the church defends its reason to exist. Knowing and following Jesus must be the priority. He will lead us to embrace His Kingdom and express it through the whole Church on earth.

# HOW DO WE COMMIT?

If commitment involves significant investment, let's use a related term to understand how. Before making any investment in life, you ought to do 'due diligence.' In other words, find out all of the aspects of the project before you commit to it:

> *Suppose one of you wants to build a tower. Will he not first sit down and estimate the cost to see if he has enough money to complete it? For if he lays the foundation and is not able to finish it, everyone who sees it will ridicule him, saying "This fellow began to build and was not able to finish."*
>
> Luke 14:28-30

Just as there is a cost to building a house, there is a cost to building your life according to the ways of God. You must be willing to walk through tough times, relate to people who are different, be exposed to people's warts, and find out that all leaders are not great leaders. If you can't handle those sorts of things, then you better stay away from the Kingdom of God.

Jesus said, *"Anyone who does not carry his cross and follow me cannot be my disciple"* (Luke 14:27). If you are only looking for self-help and solved problems, don't make a commitment to Jesus Christ, His Kingdom or His Church. You will only be disillusioned, pulling others down with you.

But, if you are willing to grow up, experience the grace of God in the tough times, and accept the mysteries you cannot understand -- if you are willing to stay in it for the long haul, then you have counted the cost. You have done due diligence. People won't be walking by your 'house' saying, "He started to build, but he failed." You won't be found in the caravan of "consumer" Christians trying to shop churches like they do shopping malls. You will be growing.

Jesus said that you cannot be a true disciple of His if you are unwilling to leave everything else behind. Value systems, relationships...everything that is not of the Kingdom of God has to be abandoned as you embrace His life.

## CONCLUSION

Commitment is indeed essential. It is at the core of the issue. It is vital to every relationship. But before you go rushing down the next aisle to recommit your life to Jesus, take a moment to ask yourself if you have done the

# A Treasure Worth the Effort

greater works. Have you truly counted the cost of discipleship? Are you ready to "take up your cross"? There is no short-term investment if you are going for the Kingdom of God. It's for the long haul.

God is calling us today to be a people who will make a steadfast commitment to follow Him. He seeks those who, in spite of the pain of failed past commitments, will say, "Commitment is a part of me; it's good; and it is a part of the life I have embraced. I am absolutely committed to Jesus Christ."

When you are more excited about knowing Christ than about fixing your problems, you are getting closer to the reality of what Christianity is meant to be. When you are willing to step out with that kind of trust, you are in for the greatest adventure of your life -- the adventure of seeing and experiencing the Kingdom of God.

*Father, place this truth deep in our hearts. Give us the courage to see that the treasure is worth the effort. Help us commit ourselves wholeheartedly to You, Your Kingdom, and Your Church. Amen.*

*The Joy of Commitment*

## ***Treasure Hunt "Clues"***
Ch. 6 -- The Joy of Commitment

1. I am afraid of commitment, having been burned in the past. How can I overcome that fear?

   Proverbs 3:5-6            Philippians 3:13-14
   Psalms 37:5               Philippians 4:4-8
   Romans 12:14-21           I John 4:13-18

2. How can God be fully committed to me, especially with my past?

   Lamentations 3:19-25      Colossians 1:19-22
   Jeremiah 31:3-4           Hebrews 13:5-6
   Romans 8:1, 8:38          I John 1:9

3. Can't I commit to God without committing to the local church and all the people?

   Romans 12:9-13            I John 4:7-8
   I Corinthians 12:12-27
   I Peter 3:8

4. What does it take for a believer to be a true disciple?

   Matthew 6:19-33
   Luke 9:23-27, 14:25-33
   Philippians 2:1-18

# 7 ‖ *Living at a Higher Level*

In an atmosphere where independence and personal rights are championed, concepts like sacrifice and discipline are not popular. But these are part of the Life that we receive from Jesus.

## BEYOND SACRIFICE

If we really understood what it means to answer the call of the Gospel, sacrifice would not be an issue. And we would see the word itself in a totally different light. We talk about sacrifice and have grandiose ideas about sacrifice. But do you realize that discipline -- self discipline -- is a form of sacrifice? We are sacrificing the choice of the "flesh" for the choice of the Spirit. I'm not talking about striving and performance, or being a martyr, but of choosing to overcome the obstacles that lie in the path toward true wholeness.

I'm talking about truly embracing love and freedom, that higher level of living to which God calls us. Discipline is the only way to real freedom. It is our personal expression of understanding the call of the Gospel, of sacrificing all for the real treasure of trading up to a higher level of freedom.

Paul explains in Galatians that *"It is for freedom that Christ set us free"* (Galatians 5:1a). God's desire is indeed freedom. But you are not really free until you can give up your rights. Yielding our rights is one of the biggest challenges to today's Christians. The modern concept of liberty seems to be having all your rights, giving up nothing, and having everything under your control.

Real freedom, however, is found in relinquishing your rights; our entitlement-driven society seems to have forgotten that. It seems we are more interested in protecting unearned rights than in looking out for the common good. The truly free person does not fight for the elusive "personal rights". He knows who he is in Christ and knows his inheritance. He is free to give, because he knows Who his security is. In Paul's view, a truly free person is able to give up those things that may be his by right, because he's motivated by a higher goal. Paul dealt with this issue in 1 Corinthians chapters 9-10:

> *If we have sown spiritual seed among you, is it too much if we reap a material harvest from you? If others have this right of support from you, shouldn't we have it all the*

*more?*

> *But we did not use this right. On the contrary, we put up with anything rather than hinder the gospel of Christ.*
> I Corinthians 9:11-12

Evidently, in Corinth at that time, the people did not want to support Paul's ministry. They under-valued his authority and ignored his physical needs. In the midst of this discourse, Paul discusses liberty, his own freedom, discipline, and their interrelationship. I believe these are things *we* need to address as well. We are facing the same attitudes, and we need to heed this relevant message.

## THE PURSUIT OF GODLINESS

Paul's concept of freedom was more than just freedom from law. It was also more than giving up personal rights. Evidently, it was a lifestyle of liberation and it was a dissatisfaction with "just getting by." To him, the liberty of real godliness was a worthy pursuit.

> *Do you not know that in a race all the runners run, but only one gets the prize? Run in such a way as to get the prize. Everyone who competes in the games goes into strict training. They do it to get a crown that will not last; but we do it to get a crown that will last forever.*
>
> *Therefore, I do not run like a man running aimlessly; I do not fight like a man*

*beating the air. No, I beat my body and make it my slave so that after I have preached to others, I myself will not be disqualified for the prize.*

I Corinthians 9:24-27

I define discipline as the choice to bring all I am responsible for under the authority of God's truth. In this passage, Paul made this choice.

A teenager asked me why God gave us the strong sexual drive and then told us to wait until marriage. I believe I answered correctly by telling her that God wants us to be overcomers. Two areas we must take authority over in our early years are our sex drive ("*Flee the evil desires of youth...*", 2 Timothy 2:22) and our thought life ("*...take every thought captive to make it obedient to Christ,*" 2 Corinthians 10:4-6). If these are allowed to run out-of-bounds, our lives will be shattered.

Just as we build physical muscles by physical exercise, we build overcomer's muscle by bringing our minds and bodily desires under the control of God's Spirit.

## CASTAWAY GRAVEYARDS

In I Corinthians 10, Paul relates a condensed narrative of Israelite history. He shows how the people were often destroyed by their defective perspectives and misplaced faith. Because they chose not to implement the proper controls in their lives, they failed in several ways. Some of them, Paul says, were idolaters. Instead of controlling their appetites, they "*sat down to eat and drink*

# A Treasure Worth the Effort

*and got up to indulge in pagan revelry"* (I Corinthians 10:7). They became castaways.

What is a castaway? It is one who has experienced God, but has chosen not to meet the challenge of bringing the body, mind, materials, and relationships under control. The passage tells us definitely how *not* to act and explains the consequences of wrong choices and lack of discipline. Those things were given to us *"to keep us from setting our hearts on evil as they did"* and were written down *"as warnings for us"* (1 Corinthians 10:6,11). It is a stern warning, yet it is followed by a powerful reassurance:

> *And God is faithful; He will not let you be tempted beyond what you can bear. But when you are tempted, He will also provide a way out so that you can stand up under it.*
> I Corinthians 10:13

We are not unique in our trials and temptations. We do have a way out in Jesus Christ. Therefore, we can choose to discipline our "fleshly mindset" through the power of the Holy Spirit. We will -- through the choices we make -- either be an overcomer or a castaway. We have a destiny as one or the other. You are probably asking, "How do I choose the overcomer's destiny rather than the castaway's; especially if I've already pretty much messed up?" We will deal with this in a later chapter. But for now:

Remember! God gives grace to those who obey. With a command, God also gives the ability to carry it out.

> *Therefore, my dear friends, as you have always obeyed--not only in my presence, but now much more in my absence--continue to*

*work out your salvation with fear and trembling, for it is God who works in you to will and to act according to his good purpose.*
                                                    Philippians 2:12-13

Remember! It is our responsibility to make the choice. It will be awkward at first. But continual "exercises" will ultimately turn the choice into a reflex.

Remember! We will never get so free that we don't need to trust God continually for His power to live.

Let's choose to avoid the castaway graveyards.

The first graveyard we need to avoid is idolatry -- putting our faith in something or someone other than God. We tend to do this when we live with a divided faith -- trusting God for spiritual things, money for financial security and people for emotional support. A good example of this is what happened because of the Israelites' impatience while Moses was up on the mountain. His seeming delay on the mountain was their occasion to transfer their trust to something they could see (the golden calf they made) while Moses was absent and God was invisible.

A second graveyard we must avoid is sexual immorality. We all know people whose illegitimate attempts to meet legitimate needs cost them their ministry, their effectiveness and their joy in life. Some have been restored, but their numbers are painfully few. We must learn to identify our legitimate needs and allow the Heavenly Father to meet them. You _will_ have sexual temptations. When you do, it is an opportunity to either overcome or become a castaway.

## A Treasure Worth the Effort

Another castaway graveyard is reached through presumption. You may want to read the example Paul cites as the Israelites journeyed around Edom and bitterly complained. When you begin to get impatient with God's way and God's timing, you are headed toward a castaway's graveyard. God has the right to do it His way and in His time. When you try to make Him fit into your schedule and satisfy your needs, you are bordering on presumption.

There are a number of examples of the fourth graveyard of grumbling. For instance, Aaron and Miriam, in Numbers 12, spoke against Moses' leadership and were duly punished. We must not allow our tongues to speak evil of God's mercy, His timing or His leaders. There is a right way to approach those who do not live godly or lead effectively, but grumbling is not it! Criticism, demeaning talk and casting doubt among their followers is a sure way to dig this castaway's grave.

If you are losing battles right now, be warned: you are losing authority. It's time to take authority over first things -- the little things -- so that you'll have an overcomer's authority to handle larger things. Discipline, remember, is the choice to bring all your responsibilities under the authority of God's truth. If we ignore the little things, we will not be able to handle the more important ones.

# DISCIPLINE DETERMINES DESTINY

Since Paul refers to bodily discipline in his discussion, we should look at its importance. How you handle your body is important to God, not just in the present, but when Jesus returns as well. The body is one of the "talents" we have been given to steward while on the earth (Matthew 25:14-30). If you're not taking charge of your body and using it according to the government of God, then you are an unfaithful servant. In fact, the Scripture actually says "*wicked servant*" (Matthew 25:26).

That term doesn't just refer to those who are abusing their body in immoral sex, drug abuse or perversion. It also includes those who selfishly indulge their own appetites instead of "*offering the parts of their body to the Lord as instruments of righteousness*" (Romans 6:11-14).

Paul specifically says in verse 27, "*I beat my body and make it my slave so that after I have preached to others, I myself will not be disqualified for the prize*". Paul is not talking about discipline simply for discipline's sake, nor is he talking about the body worship that is so prevalent in our culture (where acceptance is based on looks). He is talking about bringing his body into submission, so that he can be an overcomer in other areas as well.

There are many people whose souls are beaten down because of their failure to be a good steward over their bodies. If we are unwilling to take responsibility and authority over our bodies, we will not have authority over other aspects of our lives -- our minds, money, time, etc. If we ever get a glimpse of the glory of the treasure to be grasped, discipline will become meaningful -- not something to despise, but something to appreciate.

These obstacles exist so that we can tap into the resources of God's life in us (through Christ). It is then we

# A Treasure Worth the Effort

discover that we truly are more than conquerors and begin overcoming principalities, destroying wedges between the races, lies in the Church and wickedness in high places. However, we won't be able to touch any of it if we are unable to overcome the little things.

God works on the principle of rewarded faithfulness. He gives us something in the natural before releasing it in the spiritual. God gives us a physical, temporal body and expects us to take authority over it. Your body is not to set your agenda; that is the role of your spirit -- under the guidance of the Holy Spirit.

Paul said he was in pursuit of a goal. He was fighting to win the battle. He ran because he intended to win the prize. What was that prize? He said in Verse 23, *"I do all this for the sake of the gospel, that I may share in its blessings"* (Romans 6:23).

What were those blessings? Paul discovered blessing in sharing the gospel. He rejoiced in knowing that his life was an expression of Jesus Christ which was touching lives and redeeming men from darkness and hell. He walked in the resurrection life with Jesus Christ, shared in Christ's sufferings, and lived in communication with the Father and the Son through the Holy Spirit. Paul was telling us that the fellowship he had found in the gospel was worth the disciplined effort required.

He gladly disciplined his mind and body because he knew there was a treasure to be grasped and a castaway's grave to be avoided. Isn't it sad that this treasure has lost its allure for so many of us? To many, the quest for godly living sounds religious and boring. Yet the opposite is true.

The discipline of godly living provides the exciting challenge of, and invigorating strength for, overcoming. And overcoming is the natural exercise for people who know their resources in Christ.

# CONCLUSION

God truly wants you to be an overcomer. He offered His only Son so that you would seek a renewed life. He wants you to be free to experience the depths of His love. But He also asks for your hand in doing so...

If you believe this treasure is worth selling everything to obtain, make the choice to take authority over everything in your life. Submit your faith-life to Him. Yield your sex life to Him. Commit your tongue to Him. Please don't be one who experiences the reality of Christ and then falls in the wilderness. God's destiny for you is to be an overcomer. He would rather your name be written in the "Faith Hall" (Hebrews 11) than found in the castaway's graveyard.

> *Lord, thank you for the destiny before me and the life you offer. Thank you for setting me free to yield, instead of demand, my rights. I choose to bring all that I am responsible for under the authority of your truth, knowing that you will then enable me to overcome where it matters most. I willingly embrace your life. In Jesus' name. Amen.*

# A Treasure Worth the Effort

## *Treasure Hunt "Clues"*
Ch. 7 -- Living at a Higher Level

1. What do you mean by giving up our rights?

   > Galatians 2:20
   > Philippians 2:1-8
   > Colossians 3:3-4

2. If I bring all I am responsible for under the authority of God's truth does that mean I won't have further temptations and trials?

   > John 16:33
   > I Corinthians 10:12-13
   > James 1:2-4, 13-14

3. I can see the importance of being responsible in major things. But do little things really matter that much?

   > Luke 19:17
   > I Corinthians 10:31
   > Colossians 3:17

4. Is it really worth all this effort if I'm getting by all right?

   > Matthew 16:24-27
   > Mark 8:36
   > Luke 9:25
   > Philippians 3:7-21
   > I Timothy 6:6-10

# 8 ‖ Practicing the Process

## TRANSFORMATION IN PROCESS

Someone recently came to me asking for some help. He said, "All I'm asking is for you to help me get back on my feet." I understood what he was saying, and it was a legitimate request, but later I began thinking about that concept of help as we relate to God. Many of us mean "God, help me get over this little problem in my life, so that I can get on with independent living." If that is what we think of as the daily process of salvation, then we've missed what salvation really is.

Man was designed to live according to the blueprint of the Garden. As the Last Adam, Jesus demonstrates for us victory where the first Adam failed. That victory was found in yielding His life to God's revelation: *"For I did not speak of my own accord, but the Father Who sent me commanded me what to say and how to say it..."* (John 12:49).

If our idea of salvation is for God to get us out of trouble so we can go on living independently, or we think that we are going to progress to the point we don't need Him every moment, then we have misunderstood salvation. We need to re-evaluate and understand Who begins the work, and Who brings it to completion.

## GOD INITIATES THE PROCESS

To help us understand this daily process of salvation, let's review a story in Matthew 14. Having just finished feeding the five thousand, Jesus instructed the disciples to get into the boat and cross over to the other side while He dismissed the crowds. When Jesus was alone, He went up on a mountainside to pray.

Meanwhile, the disciples in the boat out on the lake were being buffeted by the wind and the waves. Jesus came, walking on the water, at exactly the right moment. They had given up all hope of saving the boat and their lives. Jesus immediately told them not to be afraid as He identified Himself. Peter said, *"Lord, if it is You, tell me to come to you on the water."* Jesus replied, *"Come."* Peter started out on the water and actually walked a few steps until he began to focus on the winds and the waves. Then he resorted to his natural knowledge and realized walking on water was impossible.

Fear replaced his faith in Jesus, and he began to sink. But as he began to go under, he cried out in desperation, "Lord, save me!" Jesus reached down, caught him, and took him back to the boat. I believe that when Jesus reached out to pick him up, Peter clung to Him like a child would cling to a father in that same situation. I picture an image of Jesus walking back to the boat with Peter nestled comfortably in His arms.

When they got back to the boat, the disciples were astounded by what they had just seen, and everyone in the boat worshipped Jesus. When they climbed into the boat, the wind died down. The storm was over because it had accomplished its purpose. In this story we can find some spiritual principles of how God works in our daily lives to mold us into the image of Jesus through the process of salvation.

# HE ENTICES US WITH HIS LIFE

Peter and the other disciples knew that using a boat was the only way to cross a lake of this size, since they were limited by the laws of nature. And those of them who were fishermen knew how to handle a boat in the water. But then a storm came up, greater than the disciples' abilities and resources. They fought the storm all night, unable to get to safety, finally realizing they simply did not have the resources to handle this problem.

Then Jesus came walking on the water at a distance. Why at a distance? Why didn't He immediately rush over to them, rebuke the storm, take them to safety and comfort them?  Instead, He walked by at a distance enticing them with the superiority of His life in comparison to the one they were experiencing.  They were afraid of the waves, but Jesus was walking on them.

We look at Jesus and think, "Wow, what a life!  I would like to walk on the water and have the things that frighten me under my feet.  I would really like to have the same love that caused Him to conquer in every situation, constrained Him to obey the Father, gave Him confidence to face the devil, and freed Him from fears of rejection and failure.  Wouldn't that resurrection life be incredible...the ability to heal the sick, raise the dead, make the blind to see, and cause the lame to walk?"

Instead, we find ourselves constantly beaten and buffeted by the circumstances of life.  The injustices of this world, our flesh, our families and friends -- all seem to be on a campaign against us.  Often this happens to us when we're sure we are walking in obedience to Him.  We tend to get disillusioned with God and think that He has led us here only to betray us.  Instead, it's all a divine set-up.  When everything seems hopeless, in reality He's just out of sight preparing your greatest miracle.

How do I know?  That storm didn't catch Jesus by surprise.  Nor did His disciples' attitudes and responses cause Him any alarm.  Jesus saw what was happening and He cared.  He cared enough not to alleviate their problem until they got desperate enough to be willing to live by faith.  There is something about looking at Jesus that entices us to move out of where we are, and on to where He is.  He planned it that way.

So where was Jesus?  He was on the mountain watching and praying.  They surely didn't know that; they were out there fighting the storm with everything they had. But doesn't Scripture teach that Jesus ascended back to the Father and now ever lives to make intercession for us? (Hebrews 7:25).  So, do you know what Jesus is doing today?  Regardless of where we are or how rough the storm, Jesus is on the mountain praying for us.  And I know some really good news:  He gets all of His prayers answered!

# HE ENCOURAGES US WITH HIS WORD

Peter was enticed by Jesus' incomparable life.  He wanted to be with Jesus; he wanted to walk on the waves instead of being buffeted by them.  When Jesus encouraged Peter with His Word, "*Come,*"  Peter must have thought, "This is it!  Jesus told me to come, so I must be able to do it.  I'm going!"  So he got out of the boat and actually experienced some of the miraculous power of living by the Word of God.

When we live by the Word of God we live by the reality of that Word.  Peter experienced that reality by walking on the water.  When we live by the Word of God we are no longer limited to the known natural laws of this world.  We are now limited only by the laws of the Kingdom of God -- which are not necessarily contrary to this world's laws, but are far superior to them.

Several things can happen when God sends us a

word. First, we gain encouragement because His Word is irrefutable. We learn His principles and laws, but God doesn't want us living only by principles and laws. He desires a personal relationship with us. We also gain a sense of the wonder of God's ways.

God gives us a word, and that word encourages us to step out in trusting faith. But between that Word and its fulfillment is a virtual wilderness where everything will seem contrary to the Word we've been given. In the wilderness we must learn to believe the Word despite the appearance of circumstances. God isn't trying to make us look foolish, but to teach us to be faithful.

Israel, as a wandering nation, experienced the wilderness before the fulfillment of the promise. Job too, persevered, trusting God and believing the Word when his entire life was crashing around him. It is in the wilderness that we learn to trust God; it is there that we realize God is so much greater than we imagined Him to be. The wilderness is designed to wean us away from everything except believing the promise (Deuteronomy 8:1-5).

When Jesus spoke the word "*Come!*" to Peter, there was a distance between where He was out on the water and where Peter stood back in the boat. Between Jesus and Peter there was a wilderness designed to expose anything in Peter that did not believe the Word of God. As Jesus entices us with His life and encourages us with His Word, He begins to expose our deception and unbelief.

# HE EXPOSES OUR
# DECEPTION AND UNBELIEF

Why would Jesus be intent upon exposing our deception and unbelief? Because He wants us to live in total dependence on Him. We have so deceived ourselves about our own knowledge. It is embarrassing to see how arrogant we really are to think that we can explain how God operates. For us to think that we can reduce God to a scientific formula that we discovered is like a bunch of ants trying to describe the orbiting of the planets.

Even Jesus the sinless Son of Man said, "*I myself can do nothing; I judge only what I hear*" (John 5:30). Without the Father's perspective, He didn't presume to act, think or interpret anything on this earth. Yet too often we arrogantly assume that we can reduce all of life to an explanation. It is that part of us we received when Adam and Eve ate from the tree of the knowledge of good and evil. We have a tendency to take the unexplainable and put it into something explainable, so we can control it and make it comfortable for us.

In God's discussion with Job, He basically said: "Don't try to reduce me to your understanding, Job. I am so much bigger than your mind. There are things about Me that will always cause you to live in wonder. You will never reduce me to a formula or an explanation, because I made you with a need for wonder." God is insistent on taking us beyond the explainable to living with a sense of wonder, because wonder produces worship.

One of the reasons we love children is because of their sense of wonder; think of a child's face when he sees

# A Treasure Worth the Effort

Santa Claus for the first time during the Christmas season. As we get older, we learn that it's just somebody's uncle dressed up in a red suit. However, the child experiences a magical joy in that aura of wondrous anticipation. But when we reduce Santa to Uncle John dressed in a red suit, we lose the delight. God is definitely not a myth as is Santa. Instead, God's goodness and mercies are real, and exceed our understanding to the degree that all we can do is kneel in worship. Yet as we get older, we tend to lose that child-like aura of wonder and explain everything away. God, however, is looking for that sense of wonder from us, His children, in worship.

What I am *not* saying is that Christianity is blind faith. I am saying that God's way is superior. God's way gives an answer to man's problems and gives meaning to man's life. From any other perspective, there is no meaning to life and no answer for the existence of suffering. Either there is a God Who created us and is at work in our lives drawing us to Himself, or there is no meaning in life at all.

Nowhere is this truth more important than in the wilderness. In the wasteland of despair between God's promise and His fulfillment, we are tempted to say God lied or does not exist. If you are experiencing this right now, you need to know that God controls the storms and the wilderness. He designed them so that they would expose in you that from which you need to be saved. As you learn to walk in constant exposure, you will gain the joy of experiencing daily salvation as He sets you free.

# HE EXTRICATES US
# BY HIS PRESENCE

In the midst of our exposure, He comes to us -- not to mock or shame us -- but to show us compassion. We have to admit we don't have it all together. We thought we were further along than we were, and we hate to fail. But God did not get upset when the storm came, nor did He get upset when Peter wanted to walk on the water and later began to sink. Jesus didn't shame him. He simply picked him up and brought him back.

This is a loving Father's work in our lives. Notice the compassion He shows. Jesus told the disciples to go to the other side, and like little children they took off for the other side. He went up on the mountain to watch and pray. They were never out of His sight or away from His heart. When they got in trouble, He came walking on the water. He planned for it. He prayed for it. He performed it.

We need to understand that our purpose for living is not to seek our comfort, but His exaltation. The story ends with Peter and Jesus walking back to the boat, and in the boat, they all worshipped Jesus. The storm was over. If we could get to the place where we could say, "Lord, whatever it takes, I want You to be exalted," then our daily need of salvation wouldn't be such a burden on us, and we wouldn't carry such a sense of failure. How else is Jesus going to be exalted as Savior if we don't need saving?

Jack Deere tells the story of being seated on an airplane beside a young lady who was quite an intellectual. They got into a discussion about the existence of God and the reasons for believing and not believing in Him. Jack, being quite an intellectual himself and well read in that area, debated her very well. Unfortunately, he made absolutely no progress with her, so eventually he just sat back and listened to the young lady tell her problems. Finally, after giving up any hope of winning her to faith in God, Jack simply said to her, "I see. You just need a savior, like I do." She broke in his presence, and Jack was then able to minister Jesus to her.

How will people in the world know Jesus is the Savior if they don't ever get to see Him save us from anything? How will they get a glimpse of a perfect savior if we hide all our failures and get so embarrassed about them that we act like a jerk when we fail? They wonder, "What is the difference between him and me? I'm really better off than he is, because it doesn't bother me to fail."

Do you see how contrary our religion has made us to the real life of Jesus? Does this mean I am encouraging failure? No, God has factored in enough failure into our lives to exalt the Saviorhood of Jesus Christ. My encouragement is to get a bigger perspective, a larger understanding of what God is doing in your life.

## OUR RESPONSE IS THE ISSUE

Here is the apparent process. He entices us with His life, He encourages us with His Word, He exposes our unbelief and deception, and then extricates us by His presence. It is not by a law, formula or creed -- it is by Himself. Ultimately, then, Jesus becomes our salvation, not just our Savior. When we know Him as our salvation, we refuse to live outside of His presence.

Practically, then, how should we operate in His presence? Where do we begin? It is in our desperation that we tap into the power of the Holy Spirit. Peter was desperate in the midst of the storm, because he didn't have the resources to deal with it. In our desperation, we cry out and let Jesus fulfill His Word in us. This is the process of working out our salvation.

Maybe you can't control your temper, lust or pride. Take it to the Lord! So many of us see our sins and we think, "I thought God saved me, but I'm just a jerk." No, God exposed those things in your life, so that Jesus could become salvation to you. Is Jesus patience? temperance? love without lust? Yes, He is! -- and He wants to be those things in you. Trust Jesus in you, in the person of the Holy Spirit, to change you on the inside. Simply cooperate with Him.

Some may think just trusting in Jesus is oversimplified advice for people with real problems. We can make it as complicated as we want, but ultimately if we are going to work out the salvation that God has put in us, it will have to be by faith. That is the only way.

# CONCLUSION

Here is how Jesus saves: First, He comes to us in our helplessness -- once we've quit striving. Next, He loves us unconditionally. We don't have to get fixed before He will help us or love us. And finally, He establishes His rule, His government, in our affairs.

# A Treasure Worth the Effort

We may have a problem we won't let God fix, because we are unwilling to acknowledge that it needs death and resurrection. If we want to keep struggling with our problems, He is not going to take over. But once we are willing, there is nothing that His resurrection power cannot remedy.

Remember, He knew you had this problem before it was exposed. He was on the mountain waiting for the right moment, praying for you. You are not surprising Him with your problem. He's been loving you all along, and He still loves you. Your failure does not affect His love one bit. Why not release it to him -- today?

*Lord, I acknowledge your control in my life and thank you for it. I realize I'm most deceived when I think I can do it myself. All I can say is, "Lord, save me!" I thank you and trust that you're now bringing about the ongoing process of my salvation. I welcome your work. Amen.*

## *Treasure Hunt "Clues"*
Ch. 8 -- Practicing the Process

1.  How can God be the initiator of trials if He is a God of Love?

    > Deuteronomy 8:1-5
    > Jeremiah 21:1-4
    > James 1:2-12
    > I Peter 4:12-16

2.  How is living by the Word of God living by the reality of that Word?

    > Psalms 1:1-3, Ch. 26
    > Proverbs 10:1-24
    > II Corinthians 5:7
    > Ephesians 4:1-3

4.  How can I find meaning or good in suffering?  How can that be a witness to the lost?

    > Romans 8:28-30
    > James 1:2-4
    > I Peter 1:3-7, 3:8-18

5.  I know Jesus was patient, could love without lust, etc.  But He was perfect.  Even though I'm human, how can I model that kind of life?

    > Romans 6:1-14
    > James 5:7-11
    > II Peter 1:3-11

# 9 ‖     *In the Meantime...*

There has been great confusion among believers about what we are to do until the Lord's return. There is an underlying belief that the "spiritual" work of the church (body ministry, soul winning, etc.) is separate from the "secular" work of making money, paying your bills and career development. As a result, many people feel like second-class Christians because they've not been called into ministry.

For this reason, we need to examine what our purpose is for the present. There are many who feel we should just exploit this wicked world system since it will burn up anyway when Jesus returns. I've actually heard people say, "Just run up as much debt as you possibly can, because when the rapture comes and the Christians get snatched out, then we'll just let the Antichrist pay our bills."

*In the Meantime...*

That attitude reveals a disdain for this "mudball" called Earth, as if we should have our minds on more "spiritual" things. This is not a legitimate approach to what we are supposed to be doing on Earth until our King gets back. In the Kingdom of God, we are to faithfully manage the King's possessions until He returns.

In the parable in Luke 19:11-26, Jesus gives some clues as to what real Kingdom living is all about. According to Him, the one thing we are supposed to do while we wait is: *do business.* To "do business" means we are to manage faithfully and responsibly whatever God has given us until He gets back. That is good stewardship, and it applies to far more than finances.

## FAITHFUL MANAGEMENT

Scripture relates: *"While they were listening to this, He went on to tell them a parable, because He was near Jerusalem and the people thought the Kingdom of God was going to appear at once"* (Luke 19:11). Take note of that comment. They *thought* the Kingdom of God (as they perceived it) was going to happen soon. He used this misconception in their hearts to teach them -- and us -- what our purpose should be while we await His return.

Jesus then told a parable about a man of noble birth (representing Himself) who went to a distant country to have himself appointed king and then return. Before he left, he gave each of his servants ten *minas* -- about three months' wages, saying: *"Put this money to work until I come back."* Although many of his subjects didn't want him to be their king, nevertheless he was crowned -- and soon returned home.

He then sent for the servants to find out what they had done with his money. The first servant had put it to use and earned ten more. The noble king was well-pleased and put him in charge of ten cities. The second servant, likewise, had put his to use and had earned five more. He was also commended by the master and put in charge of five cities.

But another servant came and, because he was afraid of the noble king, had hidden the money earning no return at all. This angered the king, who chastised and punished the servant -- taking his mina and giving it to the servant with ten minas.

The noble King then responded to those standing near who were amazed and frustrated. He explained: *"I tell you that to everyone who has, more will be given, but as for the one who has nothing, even what he has will be taken away."*

It is clear, then, that our noble King -- Jesus -- expects us to wisely steward His property while He is away. The only one *not* commended in this story was the one who kept, hid, and thus wasted the king's resources.

### It Began in the Garden

Stewardship began in the Garden of Eden when God created man. In Genesis 1:26 God said He put us here to manage His Earth, subdue it, and use His order to rule over it. That was the mandate for man when he was created.

The fact that man fell and sin entered into the created order does not deprive us our God-given privilege and responsibility: to manage the earth and do business with what's in our hand until Jesus returns.

Stewardship actually originates from the character of God. God Himself is a worker -- a creator. It is in His nature. In our fallen state of mind, though, we have a bad attitude toward work. We sometimes say that work is a result of the fall because that is when God told Adam and Eve they would eat their bread by the sweat of their brow. But man worked before the fall. God had given Adam the ability to manage the earth and name its species. Adam and Eve were operating with the capacity to express the nature of God upon the earth.

Someone might say, "I wonder what God is doing today?" God is doing what He is, acting in a manner consistent with His nature. When we get to Heaven, God is still going to be God; He will be working! If man is created in God's image and God restores us back to that image, guess what we will be doing? We will be working.

### It's a Measure of Maturity

Throughout all eternity there will be some kind of creative work going on, some kind of managing or stewardship going on. That's not bad, it's good -- because it fulfills you. Our problem is that we've misdefined work; many of us only work to get a paycheck. But there's a whole lot more to work than just making money.

In the parable, the king didn't ask specifics like, "How

many Bible verses did you memorize?" He asked about the man's stewardship -- how well the man used what had been left to his care. Here's what we need to face: we will be evaluated by our King not by how many religious activities we were in, but by how we handled what was given to us while He was away.

If we truly believed in the importance of good stewardship, we would be more interested in our work. We would try to make our *work* godly rather than reduce godliness to religious activities.

## YOU HAVE MUCH TO MANAGE FOR GOD

Every resource that we have is a gift given to us to be invested. The key is in the investing. One servant invested ten and gained ten more; the second invested five and earned five more. Both of them were praised and both were pleasing to the master. But the third simply hid the money -- and was rebuked for it. The issue, then, is not just in the amount of profit gained, but in the investing.

Some of us will get a better 'return' on our investment; and some will end up in more noticeable places. We are not to concentrate on the profit, but rather on how we invest. Even a poor investment is better than no investment. According to this parable, the worst thing you can do is refuse to invest. So what do we have to offer back to God? Let's examine several of the things that have been entrusted to us.

God gave us a body. It is a gift with both practical

and spiritual ramifications, which we discussed in Chapter 7. We have also been given a mind. Many have wrongly concluded that their mind is their own and they can do with it as they please. "If I don't want to educate my mind, that's my business," they say. "I don't have to learn to communicate if I don't want to. How I think is my business, and I'm content with staying the way I am." That attitude essentially says to God, "I own this thing, not You." I think some of us need to realize that God intends for our minds to be better when He gets back than when He left. We have some choices to make regarding not only what goes *into* our mind, but also *what goes on inside* of it.

Another thing we have been given is our influence. We may not have as much as we perceive other people have, but we certainly do have influence. Kids, co-workers, spouse, neighbors -- we affect them. Chances are they follow our lead in many ways. Our influence should be used to build others up, not to criticize or put them down. We are responsible for whatever reputation we have, and it's to be used for the glory of God, not for our own sake.

Our natural talents are also gifts to us. We may think they came from our parents, but it was really the sovereign plan of God to give us natural talents. It might be a gift for organization, an athletic skill, a musical talent or mental acumen. Whatever it is, it is to be stewarded faithfully. We should continually develop and invest that talent so it will grow. We're going to be judged by what God put in our hand to help us do business.

Our spiritual gifts are supernatural resources from our Heavenly Father. It is not pleasing to Him when we say things like, "Well, I just haven't been given any gifts." That

# A Treasure Worth the Effort

is a lie; it's false humility.  It is also bad stewardship, because God didn't leave any of us without spiritual gifts and He wants those gifts developed.  When the Lord tells us to express our gifts, He intends to develop our faith as we operate in them.

It takes faith to say, "God, I believe there is a gift in me, and I believe You will activate it when I get out there and start expressing it."  It takes faith to move out.  A fledgling prophet or teacher, or someone learning to show hospitality, is only going to become proficient by venturing out and using it.

Our fear of failure keeps us from investing because we are afraid the venture won't turn out, we won't perform well, or we will be laughed at -- even rejected -- by others.  God wants to free us from that hideous fear.  We may want to believe God for great miracles and influential ministries, but if we are unwilling to step out and act in the little things, He won't release to us the greater tasks.

Stewardship is a definable concept.  Being a good steward over what God has given us is the way we express our love back to Him.  Jesus gave us the way to evaluate our own heart: if we love Him, we will keep His commands.  We need to find out what Jesus wants us to do and do it: *"Whoever has my commands and obeys them, he is the one who loves me.  He who loves me will be loved by my Father, and I too will love him and show myself to him"* (John 14:21).

*In the Meantime...*

# STEWARDSHIP IN
# A HOSTILE ENVIRONMENT

We need to remember that we have been left to do business in a hostile environment. In the parable, the king's subjects did not want him to be king, even to the point of attempting political maneuvers to try to prevent it. We, too, live in such an environment: the subjects don't want Jesus to be King. They have tried to obliterate His laws and to take away His right to govern. You and I live in that atmosphere and it is easy to be affected by it.

It should be clear, then, that we cannot trust the value system of a culture who hates their King. Therefore, we must always be on the alert to discern the difference in the laws of the Kingdom of God and the laws of the kingdom of this cultural system. We cannot blindly allow the world to teach us its economics, its politics, its way of defining values, and its way of handling money.

The truth of the harvest is that we will reap what we sow. We will be blessed according to the resources of God's Kingdom, if that's the King we choose to serve. Likewise, we cannot live contrary to the laws of God's Kingdom and expect that kingdom to deposit its resources in our account. The truth is, we're going to benefit from whichever kingdom we serve.

# STEWARDSHIP YIELDS INCREASE

Do you want more? Use what you have better! That's the bottom line. Increased responsibility, increased authority, more finances -- these are all based upon stewardship. The answer is not in how much we beg and plead, or how "competitive" we are spiritually. It is found in how well we handle what God has given us.

Increase is based on stewardship. If we are not increasing in an area of our life, we need to evaluate our management of that area. What are we doing to bring God greater glory? In what ways are we keeping back that which is rightfully His? We can't look around for someone else to blame. The wicked servant couldn't face his own mis-management, and instead wanted to blame it on the character of the king.

The true character of the king, however, had already been expressed when the king gave the servant three months' wages to work with. He said in effect, "I give it to you to do business with; it belongs to me, but I want you to manage it." That is the true character of our King. If we believe the best about our King and are good stewards over what He has given us, then we won't act like victims and inhibit the flow of increase in our lives.

## CONCLUSION

Stewardship is a great privilege. In the Kingdom of God, we are to do business until the King gets back. Our increase in every area of life is in proportion to our stewardship. God designed it that way because He wants us to grow up to participate in His character. It takes more wisdom, perseverance, faith and grace than we possess to be a good steward. Therefore, we must learn how to trust

*In the Meantime...*

God for His resources to get the job done.

God wants us to grow from being little children into overseers in the "family business." We're not talking about earning our way into heaven or even earning blessings; we are talking about participating with God in His kingdom.

Make use of what you have; God promises He will give you more. If you need revelation, then respond to what you have already been given. Our problem is not that we need more of anything; our problem is negligence concerning what we already have.

*Father, thank You for the privilege of participating in Your Kingdom. We want to know how your government works in order to better manage the earth. Take this truth and guide it around all our mental road blocks -- fear of legalism, fear of failure, and pride. Thank you for being persistent in helping us grow up. In Jesus' name, Amen.*

# A Treasure Worth the Effort

## *Treasure Hunt "Clues"*
### Ch. 9 -- In the Meantime

1. How should I view work?

   | | |
   |---|---|
   | Exodus 20:9-10 | I Corinthians 3:10-15 |
   | Psalms 62:11-12, 90:17 | I Thessalonians 4:11-12 |
   | John 5:17, 9:4 | II Thessalonians 3:10-13 |

2. Why is our stewardship of everything so important?

   Genesis 1:26-30
   Malachi 3:8-12
   Luke 19:11-26
   I Corinthians 6:12-20

3. Isn't gaining knowledge being a good steward of my mind?

   | | |
   |---|---|
   | Genesis 2:17 | Ephesians 3:14-19 |
   | Psalms 119:65-66 | Philippians 1:9-11 |
   | Proverbs 1:4-7, 2:1-11 | Colossians 1:9 |
   | Romans 8:1b-3 | |

4. Isn't it a bad "witness" if I venture out to try something and make a mess of it?

   Romans 8:1
   Colossians 1:27
   Philippians 3:12-14

5. If it's all God's, why does he let the "world system" control so much of it?

   Romans 7:5, 7:8
   James 4:1-10
   I John 2:6-17

# 1 0 | *It's Worth the Effort!*

We have sought throughout this book not only to find, but also to experience the treasure that awaits the child of God. Along the pathway we have learned to discern between the "costume" jewelry -- which looks real but is not, and the real jewels -- treasure that is pure and valuable; lasting.

Real treasure -- jewels, gold and silver -- is brought to its purest and most brilliant state when subjected to pressure, heat, or the "chisel". So too, the child of God. These words themselves sound hard and negative. In fact, we immediately sense pain and discomfort just hearing them. And sometimes the experiences surrounding them feel just that way.

Yet Scripture tells us time and again to "*Consider it pure joy...,*" and "*You are blessed...*" (James 1:2-4,12); to

# A Treasure Worth the Effort

*"Rejoice always...,"* and *"In all circumstances give thanks...,"* (I Thessalonians 5:16-18); *"In this you greatly rejoice..."* (I Peter 1:3-7).

There must be something significant that we are missing then, if we always look at these situations with fear and dread. A review of Romans 8:28-30 will help us. Don't just stop at verse 28!

> *And we know that in all things God works for the good of those who love him, who have been called according to this purpose. For those God foreknew he also predestined to be conformed to the likeness of his Son, that he might be the firstborn among many brothers. And those he predestined, he also called; those he called, he also justified; those he justified, he also glorified.*
>
> Romans 8:28-30

This is good! This is treasure!

## THE TREASURE HUNT

Did you ever watch a movie where they were searching for lost treasure? They didn't hop into an air-conditioned car with a stereo CD player, ride a couple miles, hop out and pick up a treasure chest full of gold, silver and jewels.

They usually had one of the following scenarios: They had to cross a desert encountering snakes, extreme heat, had little to no water, got lost once or twice and almost died.  Or, they hacked their way through the jungle, subject to all sorts of wild animals (including each other), disease, cuts and bruises, and almost died.  Or they sailed across the ocean in a ship whose crew consisted of 30 men -- all prisoners who hated each other, and all of whom hated the captain -- had at least two mutinies and one terrible storm, in which the ship almost sank.  And they almost died.  Then, just before giving up entirely, or at death's door, they stumbled upon the hidden treasure.

This is really a great visual explanation of Scripture. The thing most valuable may be the hardest to find -- not because God makes it hard, but because *we* do.  We struggle through on our own, we fight God at almost every turn (quietly or openly) and we get to the point of desperation (death).  Then we stumble upon the treasure -- God is the source, the strength, the Life.  *"It is the glory of God to conceal a matter; to search out a matter is the glory of kings"* (Proverbs 25:2).

Our physical and spiritual focus and vision make all the difference.  Focusing on self is fear and bondage -- the "costume" jewelry.  Focusing on God is trust and love -- the *real* treasure.

## THE JOURNEY

If we understand that the journey itself is as important as the destination, we will save much wear and tear on our souls as well as our bodies.  There is more to trip planning than just the destination.  You need to know and plan for several things.  What is the best route?  How

# A Treasure Worth the Effort

long will it take? What provisions are needed? What is the cost? What are the backup plans in case of trouble?

Once these are determined and you start the trip -- whether you take a plane, bus, ship or drive a car -- there are certain rules you must follow -- absolutes that can't be changed. You cannot decide that you will sit in the pilot's seat and fly the plane if you are a passenger. If you are driving, you cannot decide that you will drive in a field beside the highway instead of in your proper lane inside the painted lines as the law requires.

Yes, you live in a free country and you are free. And you have the choice of breaking the law and endangering the lives of others. However, some choices will yield bondage, death and destruction.

Likewise, if you are in California and want to go to New York, it would be silly to go west from California instead of east. Yes, you would finally get there. But it would cost you much more, take much longer and would be much more wear and tear on you physically, mentally, and probably emotionally.

Apply these examples to our journey called *life*. We have a "road map" and a Guide who has all the resources and provisions we need. The cost is *our* life, but the backup plan is *His Life*. God has given us Jesus Christ. In His life there are absolutes. If we live within those absolutes there is more freedom than we can imagine. If we live outside of these absolutes in what the world calls freedom -- humanism and its philosophy of relativism -- we "exist" in bondage and deception. And it costs us our lives - with no backup plan.

*It's Worth the Effort!*

You have a choice to represent Jesus Christ. With that choice, you identify your target -- affecting our culture by living the Gospel, whether in a one-on-one setting or in a large-group setting. That identification produces areas that cannot be compromised in your life. You know there is a Sovereign God who cannot lie. He has spoken and it is all truth. If you have made these choices, there is only one thing that flows naturally from this -- obedience.

# FINDING JEWELS ALONG THE WAY

Christians are not exempt from struggles -- sometimes severe struggles. These are part of the maturing process, a process that moves us toward a greater understanding and expression of love. Our real maturity comes when we learn to love God and others for their sake and not our own.

Experiencing this kind of love frees us from using our defective "emotional programs for happiness" to meet our needs. As we exalt Jesus instead of focusing on ourselves, we have found one of the jewels of the treasure.

Do we understand how much God really loves us? If so, our view of His discipline will change. We will receive it as the encouraging, developing tool He uses, in love, for our good. He sees the whole picture and knows where He wants to take us. We see only the "now" and don't always understand.

This process is not an overnight deal. As much as we would like to "blink" and have the tough times gone, there are no shortcuts. The easy way out will leave you empty -- your soul will be lean, without peace and joy.

# A Treasure Worth the Effort

You will not develop wisdom and discernment or know the ways of the Lord.

The truth is, the easy way out is really the hard way out. What we try to escape we will actually be running toward. The wisdom of the world will give you deception, confusion, selfishness, jealousy, disorder and "*every evil thing*". This wisdom is demonic.

Wisdom from above will give you a "*harvest of righteousness and peace*" (Hebrews 12:11). All of Scripture, especially Proverbs, is full of the benefits and blessings of gaining wisdom. This is the refined gold for our treasure.

Surely there is no contest here. Either choice will have it's struggles. Both lead to death. But only one death actually results in life -- Christ's Life in us.

## COMMITTED TO THE TASK

Are we willing to make that commitment? Are we willing to yield our rights, walk in obedience and know "*the fellowship of sharing in His sufferings*" (Philippians 3:10)? If He learned obedience through suffering, should we expect less? He was committed beyond His own desires to do only what the Father said do. How can we think we know it all and disregard obedience?

He poured Himself into the twelve disciples, then was close to the seventy, then preached to the masses. Is that a model for us? Are we committed intimately to a few or a small group, then on a broader scale within the local expression of the Body of Christ, then to the Church at large?  Or do we stay in a protective cocoon of selected "like" people and activities, away from those who are different and difficult.  If we are isolated, we are self-focused.

To be committed to Jesus is to be committed to the Kingdom of God, which is to be committed to His Church. It must flow in this order or it will become legalistic, Pharisaical and territorial.  Commitment to Jesus is the priority.  Through that commitment, He will guide us in expressing our lives in His Kingdom and through His Church.  Committing is like planning for the trip -- you must know your negotiables and non-negotiables, count the cost, and then "go for it"!

## OVERCOMING "ROADBLOCKS"

Committing requires sacrificing our *flesh* and choosing the way of the Spirit. It is pressing on toward the prize (treasure) of the higher life that God is calling us to. It is overcoming.  To sacrifice is to exercise self-discipline and to yield our rights.  This seems initially to be a difficult and unpopular choice.  Yet it is the pathway to real freedom and security.

God has given us many "talents" to manage -- our bodies, minds, time, money, etc.  He expects us to steward these talents in His behalf while He is away.  And He will reward us accordingly when He returns.

While the discipline we exercise over these talents may not seem pleasant at the moment, it will gain for us *"an eternal glory that far outweighs them all"* (II Corinthians

4:17) in the long run. Our reward is not just later on. As we overcome in this process, He will give us increased authority in greater areas. We are beginning to see the value of this treasure.

We learn also in the process that we can do nothing without His constant grace -- His empowering presence. This realization, that it is Christ -- and only Christ, is a "pearl of great price" added to our treasure.

Think about what we have talked about. We have a Sovereign God who loves us and is intimately involved with us. He is pouring out His grace and sufficiency as He is taking us through the custom-made experiences He knows will purify, edify and build us into all that He desires for us to be -- faithful sons and daughters.

He loves us enough to expose and remove (if we allow Him to) our deception and unbelief. Yet He loves us too much to leave us floundering until we "get it right". He is always there. He has given us Jesus' life to be expressed through His Holy Spirit. How can we dare assume that we can do it on our own!

## SHARING OUR TREASURE

As we navigate our pathway toward wholeness, we show a lost and dying world what it means to have a Savior. What will draw them or turn them away is how we deal with all our messes and failures. That doesn't mean we will act as if we are perfect; but if they see Jesus, they will come.

*It's Worth the Effort!*

We share our life, our "ministry", wherever we are. We all have a mission field, whether in an office, at home, or in the Church. We should not think in terms of *secular* work and *Christian* work. It is all God's; we are His children, and wherever we are, He is. We are to "do business" His way in whatever we do. That's how God started it with Adam, and He hasn't changed it since. When He returns that will be His measure for rewards -- how did we manage what He gave us responsibility over, not what religious activities we accomplished.

What are we doing with our bodies, our minds, our finances, our influence, our natural talents and our spiritual gifts? Will He say, "Well done, good and faithful servant"? If so, He will give us an increase -- in wisdom, grace, and authority. We will have found the treasure, and can joyfully lay it at His feet.

# CONCLUSION

The treasure God has offered us in the Gospel is so incredibly wonderful, that it makes whatever sacrifice it costs a bargain. If you have not found this treasure that is worth everything, keep searching! Once you find the beauty of God's promises and embrace His Kingdom, all else pales in comparison. You will gladly sell everything you have in order to get it:

*The kingdom of heaven is like treasure hidden in a field. When a man found it, he hid it again, and then in his joy went and sold all he had and bought that field.*

Matthew 13:44

## A Treasure Worth the Effort

If you gain nothing else from reading this book, I hope for your sake that you will grasp the meaning of Jesus' description in this passage. The treasure He spoke of is worth whatever effort is required to obtain it. PRESS ON!

*Father, teach me the true value of living Your Life. Thank you for guiding me safely this far; I trust you now to lead me home. Show me where to begin, and keep me pressing on toward your goal.*

*Amen.*

# A Treasure Worth the Effort

## References Cited

1. Peterson, Eugene  The Message (NavPress, 1993).

2. Murray, Andrew, Ed.  Wholly For God: Selections From the Writings of William Law (Minneapolis, MN: Dimensions Books / Bethany Fellowship, Inc., 1976).

3. Chesterton, G. K.  "On Certain Modern Writers and the Institution of the Family" in The Collected Works of G. K. Chesterton, David Dooley, Ed. (San Francisco, CA: Ignatius Press, nd.), pp. 136-137.

# Other Books By Dudley Hall

Jesus is preparing new wineskins for the new wine He is pouring throughout His Church. This book helps you confront the fears and lessens the pain from coming "out of the comfort zone."

$9.00

If you are tired of struggling, feeling guilty and never measuring up, let the message of grace breathe life back into you. Step out of the complexities of religion into a simple but passionate love relationship with God.

$11.00

## *Christian Maturity Series*

Life on the highest plane requires an energy that is only released when love is awakened. Passionless living will never produce holiness nor liberty. However, life with passion will bring a fullness that liberates and satisfies.

$7.00

Christian growth is the process of "trading up." When there is a treasure to be found, even the search can be exhilarating. God has offered a life worth the search if you know where to look and how to trade up and obtain it.

$7.00

Prayer is not only the opportunity to fellowship with God, but a partnership with Him. As we send up prayer (incense), He answers back with expressions of His power (thunder). When we engage in prayer from this perspective, we experience heaven affecting earth.

$7.00

## Books By T.D. Hall

This study guide is an excellent tool to help strengthen believers—especially new converts—about the things that are truly ours as Christians.

$5.00

Biblical encouragement and information to help us develop and express the love of Jesus Christ to one another.

$4.00

# "Living the Life" Tape Series
## By Dudley Hall     $20.00 / set

Dudley has recently put together several new tape sets we think you'll enjoy. These are topical study collections of some of Dudley's most popular monthly messages. This would be a great way to catch-up on previous messages as well as introduce family and friends to some practical biblical teaching. Try them, we think you'll like them! To place your order, call: 1-800-530-4933.

## PURCHASE 3 SETS & RECEIVE THE 4TH SET FREE!

### Life At It's Best
- Passionate Living
- Life in the Word
- Discovering Your Own Ministry
- Sharpening Your Discernment

### God's Masterpiece The Emerging Church
- The Transitional Church
- What is Church Life?
- New Day, New Leaders
- High Impact Christianity

### Meeting Life's Crisis
- Grace Applied to Failure
- Forgiveness—The Key to Deliverance
- Real Faith Will Last
- What to Do While You Wait

### Seeking Life's Treasure
- Kingdom Consciousness
- Simplicity
- Being the Salt of the Earth
- Living in God's Today
- Seeing the Kingdom
- Life and Peace

### Breaking the Grip of Dead Religion
- Exposing Self-Righteousness
- Escaping Legalism
- The Offense of Simplicity
- Mature Thinking

### Building a Storm Proof Life
- Building on the Rock vs Sand
- Protecting the Mind
- Blessed Are the Unoffended
- Authority and Power

### The Art of Hearing God
- Hearing God
- How Did Jesus Hear?
- Intimacy
- Tuning You Spiritual Ears
- Learning to Listen

### Winning in the Game of Life
- A New Look At Holiness
- How Does God Motivate?
- Focus on the Main Thing
- Walking in Integrity
- "Follow" is a Good Word
- Living in the Presence

# Dudley Hall's Monthly Message

**Have you heard about . . .** Dudley Hall has a uniquely refreshing ministry of grace and restoration. "He makes the essential things seem simple" is a common remark from one who has heard Dudley speak. If you want a no-nonsense approach to living, you will benefit from these messages. While you laugh and sometimes cry, truth will grip you in such a practical way that you are encouraged to put it into practice.

From a background of religion substituted for life, Dudley shares a message of grace and simplicity. Liberation from legalism as well as total involvement in the Kingdom of God give balance to a message designed to fulfill our destiny in Christ.

Literally thousands have been deeply touched. Many have been receiving monthly tapes and outlines for years. They have found a trustworthy resource and value it.

This is not just a program of random messages selected to impress people or promote sales. It is a "life in process" being shared through a craftsman's skill and disciple's heart. We hope you try it, we think you'll like it!

--------------------------------------------------------------

# SCLM ORDER FORM
### MAIL ORDER TO:
### SCLM, PO BOX 101, EULESS TX 76039
### SEE CHART FOR SHIPPING & HANDLING CHARGES

NAME _____

ADDRESS_____

CITY_____ST_____ ZIP_____

PHONE_____

**VISA/MASTER CARD ORDERS: CALL 1-800-530-4933**
**MONDAY-FRIDAY, 8:00 A.M. TO 5:00 P.M. (CST)**
**$10 MINIMUM ORDER REQUIRED ON CHARGES**
**PLEASE CHARGE TO MY VISA/MASTER CARD:**

NO._____EXP. DATE _____

SIGNATURE_____

AVAILABILITY & PRICES SUBJECT TO CHANGE WITHOUT NOTICE.
ONLY U.S. CURRENCY ACCEPTED FOR PAYMENT.
ALLOW 4 TO 6 WEEKS FOR DELIVERY.

| # | ITEM | EA | TOTAL |
|---|------|-----|-------|
| | | | |
| | | | |
| | | | |
| | | | |
| | | | |
| | | | |
| | | | |
| | | | |
| | SHIPPING & HANDLING | | |
| | TOTAL | | |

### SHIPPING & HANDLING FEES:

| ITEMS | TOTAL | U.S. FEE | OTHER COUNTRY |
|-------|-------|----------|---------------|
| BKS / TAPES SETS | $0-$10 | $2.00 | $3.50 |
| | $11-$30 | $3.75 | $5.50 |
| | $30 & UP | $5.50 | $7.50 |